Dollhouse Furniture
You Can Make

Ruth Glick • Nancy Baggett

Photographs by Charlie C. Baggett, Jr.
Illustrations by Christine P. Tischer

South Brunswick and New York: A. S. Barnes and Company
London: Thomas Yoseloff Ltd

Dollhouse
Furniture
You Can Make

A. S. Barnes and Co., Inc.
Cranbury, New Jersey 08512

Thomas Yoseloff Ltd
Magdalen House
136-148 Tooley Street
London SE1 2TT, England

Library of Congress Cataloging in Publication Data

Glick, Ruth, 1942-
    Dollhouse furniture you can make.

    SUMMARY: Presents step-by-step directions for building
a doll house and using household items to make furniture,
accessories, and appliances.
    1. Doll furniture. [1. Doll furniture. 2. Doll-
houses] I. Baggett, Nancy, 1943- joint author.
II. Baggett, Charlie C.   III. Tischer, Christine P.
IV. Title.
TT175.5.G54   754.59'23   76-50189
ISBN 0-498-01994-2

PRINTED IN THE UNITED STATES OF AMERICA

Acknowledgments

Many people provided encouragement and help in the preparation of this book. However, we would like to give special thanks to a number of individuals — starting with our artists. Not only did they provide an appealing visual presentation for our ideas, but they were great to work with. Charlie Baggett, our photographer, spent hours making sure each photograph would be just right. And Christine P. Tischer, our illustrator, brought our thumbnail sketches to life and made hard-to-describe directions easy to understand.

Norman Glick helped us purge the manuscript of spelling and typographical errors before it was sent to the publisher. Lawrence Tarbell developed a great set of dollhouse plans for the last chapter of our book. And Evelyn Bradford gave us the confidence to undertake such an extensive project.

And then there were all our friends and relatives — especially Delilah Jones and Beverly Burtnick — who made suggestions and emptied out their cupboards and catchall drawers to give us scores of tiny items we were able to turn into dollhouse treasures.

Introduction

There's magic in miniaturization, especially for children. Tiny reproductions of life-size objects provide a world where little people can feel at home.

That's why youngsters love dollhouses. Within the scaled-down walls they can hold dinner parties, care for the baby in the nursery, and endlessly rearrange the furniture. They can practice being grownups in their own private domain.

To open up this make-believe world for some special child, you *could* buy a dollhouse and equip it from the toy store; but, unfortunately, the dollhouses and furnishings available today are either beautiful and expensive or shoddy looking and not really a bargain.

Your alternative is to make the furniture and even the dollhouse yourself. It's easier than you might think.

To put together sturdy and attractive dollhouse furnishings, all you need is imagination and a few basic cutting, gluing, and sewing skills. Savings are enormous because all of the materials required are either inexpensive or discarded household items.

Projects in this book vary in the amount of construction time and skill they require; but since step-by-step directions are given, most of the furniture and appliances are not really difficult to make. Just be sure to read through all the steps before beginning to work. That way you'll be familiar with the entire process when you start.

As each new construction technique is introduced, easy pieces are presented first, followed by more complicated ones. If you have limited handicraft experience, you may want to start with some of the more simple projects and "work up" to the harder ones. All designs are on the scale of one inch to one foot.

This book is primarily about making furniture; but in case you want to build the dollhouse, too, plans and directions are included in the last chapter. You *will need* plywood and some carpentry ability and tools to complete the house.

It's a lot of fun to turn out tiny replicas of life-size objects. With each new creation, your children will be more enchanted. And, who knows, you may start off furnishing a dollhouse for a favorite youngster and end up playing with it yourself!

Contents

to
Elissa, Ethan, and David —
our inspiration and our best critics.

1

How to Get Started

*F*inding the materials for making dollhouse furniture and accessories is easy. Just turn on your imagination and start rummaging — in the sewing box, the bottom of the bedroom closet, and in the kitchen catchall drawer. What you've come to think of as junk may turn out to be a dollhouse treasure.

Examine everything with new eyes. Begin by studying the basic design and form of small items. And think small. In other words, say to yourself, "If I were a Lilliputian, what would *this* be?"

Take the shape of a lipstick tube, for example. The cylindrical cover is a decorative little umbrella stand. Shirt studs are attractive brass candlesticks (see figure 1). Small compartmented boxes are simple bookcases. And a hinged, plastic, straight-pin box is a kitchen wall cabinet.

If you can't visualize an item as a miniature piece of furniture or accessory, try seeing it as a part of something. A matchbox can be a desk drawer. A round cork coaster is a perfect dollhouse tabletop. And a popsicle stick is a board from a tiny picnic table. Turned with the narrow edge up, the same stick becomes a strip of butcher-block top.

You may have to disassemble some objects to appreciate their possibilities. Salvage the wire around a champagne bottle cork. Snip out the horizontal bottom wire to produce a ready-made set of chair legs. Cut the bottom from a discarded liquid-detergent bottle to use as an old-fashioned bathtub. Remove the metal cylinder from the middle of a mechanical pencil to form the base of a modern table lamp. Or dismantle

FIG. 1: Victorian parlor featuring curved-back sofa and ornate grandfather's clock.

an old light socket. The bottom cup can be turned into a brass, Tiffany-style shade (shown in figure 2).

Construction materials are all around. Everything from paper doilies and toothpaste boxes to fabric remnants, telephone wire, and olive "trees" can be turned into miniature furnishings. To help you get started collecting, here are some suggestions on what to save:

Metal

tiny screws and nuts
paper clamps
champagne cork wires
lamp sockets
parts from ball-point pens
jewelry parts
lipstick tubes
pop-out can lids
map pins
wire scraps
hook-and-eye sets and similar fasteners

12

FIG. 2: *A comfortable sitting room decorated with an assortment of modern furnishings.*

Wood

beads
dowels
small pieces of scrap lumber
toothpicks
popsicle sticks
spools
balsa strips

Plastic

tube and bottle caps
buttons and beads
bleach and other plastic bottles
styrofoam spools

Fabric and Stuffing

thin carpet samples
nylon stockings
string, thread, and wool
cloth remnants
rick-rack, braid trim, heavy lace trim, and gathered eyelet lace
foam-rubber pieces and scraps
fake fur

Paper

matchboxes
doilies
old magazines and catalogs
small cardboard boxes
wallpaper samples
wrapping paper
shoe boxes

Glass

small mirrors
beads

Odds and Ends

parts from board games
small seashells
children's blocks
charms
leftover paint

If you're not naturally a pack rat and haven't a ready assortment of junk available, don't worry. All of this paraphernalia doesn't have to be on hand to get started. Thumb through the book and pick out a project or two to try; assemble only the materials specifically required for each. You can gradually collect additional items.

Yard and garage sales are good places to look for supplies. Friends are also an excellent source. Just mention your dollhouse project, and they'll jump at the chance to provide materials. After all, how often can they clean out their closets and do a good deed for someone else at the same time?

The tools needed are minimal. Most, like scissors, pliers, and ruler, will probably be on hand. You may have to buy tin snips and a knife with disposable blades (an X-acto or razor-blade knife will do).

When you begin making your dollhouse furniture, set up a work-storage area. If necessary, this can be as simple as a card table with cardboard boxes shoved underneath. Whatever the arrangement, it will prevent materials and tools from getting scattered and misplaced and will help keep the construction process enjoyable.

Once you begin to use this book, you'll notice that chapters are arranged by building materials, such as wood, metal, plastic, or cardboard. This lets you concentrate on only one type of construction process at a time, developing expertise with the tools and materials needed. And you can put away that set of supplies when you're finished.

On the other hand, you won't find all the chairs in one chapter and all the kitchen equipment in another. To locate specific appliances or pieces of furniture, look in the index.

2

Coordinating and Decorating

*I*n a way, a dollhouse is a dream house — not only for the child who will play with it, but also for the adult who helps do the furnishing. Think about the possibilities for a moment — an entire house, completely empty and waiting for someone to bring it to life.

No wonder making your own furniture is such an exciting adventure. You can choose *exactly* the styles, the colors, the patterns, and even the textures you and your child want to enliven the tiny rooms.

Whether your taste runs to the traditional or the very modern, this book has many projects that will help carry out your ideas. It is possible to stick with one style (like the rooms shown in the photographs in chapter 1). Or, for an equally attractive look, mix and match the way professional decorators often do (figure 3 and plate 1).

But regardless of your preferences, be sure to give dollhouse decorating some careful thought.

Sit down for a conference with the proud owner of the home. And browse through the chapters of this book. Look at the furniture styles and the sample rooms. Your youngster may have very definite ideas about furnishing and decorating.

The two of you need to think about fabric choices for upholstery and window treatments, as well as for floor and wall coverings. And talk about what purpose each of the rooms will serve. Obviously your dollhouse needs a kitchen and a bathroom; but do you plan to have a study, a playroom, a combined family and dining room, or a laundry room? And how many dolls will be "living" in the house? This decision

FIG. 3: Mix traditional and modern furnishings to come up with an attractive eclectic living room.

should be made before you start assigning and decorating bedrooms. It will also determine the number of chairs you need in the dining room and the number of towel racks near the bathtub.

Many youngsters are fascinated with the prospect of making the dollhouse look as much like their own home as possible. So you may simply decide to duplicate the functions and decoration in your life-size rooms.

On the other hand, you might let some of the furniture projects in this book suggest a decorating treatment. If your child falls in love with a particular piece — the canopy bed, ornate bookcase, armoire, or modern sofa, for instance — it could become the focal point of a room. The rest of the furnishings would then be chosen to complement the featured item.

Keep in mind that even in the most spacious dollhouse — like the one presented at the end of this book — the rooms are proportionally smaller than in a real home. Not too many real dining areas are only nine feet by nine feet. But a lot of dollhouse dining rooms are nine inches by nine inches.

Therefore, to avoid an overstuffed, cluttered look, resist the temptation to crowd too many large, dramatic pieces into any one setting. And don't forget that a dollhouse room usually has only three walls. This is a further limitation on furniture placement.

It is a good idea to start by making a few essential or desired items. Others can be added later.

After furniture choice and placement, color should be your most important decorating tool. The simplest approach is to use one color scheme throughout the entire house; for example, a pastel motif. But it may be more fun to let each room make its own individual statement. The dining room and the kitchen could be in sunny oranges. And the living room could be in cool blues and greens. Or you might prefer just the reverse.

Whatever plan the two of you decide on, remember that colors must complement each other to give a well-decorated, finished look.

In dollhouse decoration, the easiest place to begin is with fabric selection — for curtains and upholstered pieces. To hang right, curtains must be of *very* lightweight material, such as dotted swiss, thin broadcloth, voile, acetate, open-weave cotton knit, or nylon.

"Upholstery fabric" needs to be opaque and durable. Medium-weight cottons and cotton-polyester blends are perfect. Lightweight polyester knits can be used in some projects. For all fabric, keep the patterns small. A one-inch square plaid that appears discreet in normal use will be gigantic in a dollhouse setting.

Small linear designs such as plaids, houndstooth and window-pane check, and stripes are handy because you can use the lines as guides during cutting and construction. As an added benefit, they can contribute a casual pattern and color interest without necessarily limiting you to a decorating period. In contrast, many small floral prints will definitely suggest a traditional or Early American theme.

Check through your own fabric scraps, ask your friends, or sort through the remnant baskets in yard-goods stores. Because of dollhouse scale, a whole room can be decorated with just a few pieces of leftover material.

When planning your decor, also think about walls and floors. Do you prefer papered or painted rooms? Do you like bare floors and throw rugs, or would you choose wall-to-wall carpeting?

Dollhouse walls can be finished with leftover interior house paint. If individual living areas are small, pale colors will make them appear larger.

Walls could also be covered with attractive wrapping paper (the type sold in rolls, not folded in squares) or adhesive-backed shelf paper. Or ask your local dealer for discontinued books of wallpaper samples. These come in a number of textures — ranging from fuzzy flocks and linen-type weaves to smooth, wet-look, vinyl finishes. The texture chosen will go far in creating the atmosphere you want.

With one sheet from most sample books, you can probably cover an accent wall. Then use a neutral paper or paint on the others. Keep scale in mind here, too. Generally, tiny patterns or stripes work best. But you may be able to produce a very dramatic effect by using a larger motif; for instance, a small scene in regular room scale will make a whole mural in a dollhouse.

Various choices are also available for floor coverings. Simulate wood flooring with "butcher block," self-adhesive paper. For the look of very expensive ceramic tile, select wallpaper with an appropriate geometric design.

Area rugs can be made from velour and patterned washcloths. Or use remnants of low-pile "fake fur." For plush wall-to-wall carpeting, choose a napped material such as no-wale corduroy or suitable upholstery fabric. An unused strip of bathroom carpeting is another alternative.

After these basic selections are made, you can start on some of the furniture projects, creating pieces to fit the settings you have in mind.

As each room begins to fill with furniture and decorations, your dollhouse will really become a home in miniature.

3

Furniture from Cloth and Stuffing

*I*n many dollhouses, the most disappointing furnishings are the sofas, chairs, and beds. Instead of feeling soft and inviting, like real upholstered pieces and bedding, they're often hard and unyielding to the touch — even when they're covered with a thin veneer of fabric.

Fortunately, when making these pieces of furniture by hand, you can create items that not only look comfortable but also feel cushion soft.

Some of the projects in this chapter, like the pillows and lounge sofa featured in figure 4, are just cloth envelopes filled with padding. For more elaborate projects, like the sofas shown in figure 5, a simple cardboard frame is first constructed. This is covered with fabric and topped by a pillow stitched across the middle to resemble four separate cushions.

With relatively few materials and techniques, many styles are possible. The key to this variety is in the great selection of fabrics you can use. Cover a simple sofa with a small chintz pattern, and it will look traditional. Upholster the same basic couch with a bold geometric print, and it will be decidedly modern in character. Pick a paisley or neutral design, and the piece will fit in almost any setting. (Since fabric selection is so important, you may want to refer back to chapter 2, ["Coordinating and Decorating,"] before picking out any "upholstery material.")

All of the projects in this chapter can be made from fabric remnants. For large pieces, such as sofas, you will need at least a half-yard of material. For smaller items, such as pillows and chairs, you can often make use of sewing-box scraps.

Check any fabric you select for flaws and misprints. And press out wrinkles before cutting.

FIG. 4: *Use pillows and a simple lounge sofa to create this informal living area.*

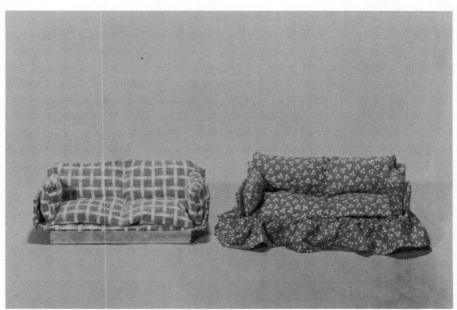

FIG. 5: *Two different sofas — one basic design! Just choose a wooden or skirted base for a modern or traditional look.*

21

The majority of projects that follow utilize simple sewing and/or gluing techniques. Generally, when gluing is necessary, a white household glue, such as Elmer's, should be used. When sewing is required, seams can be joined by hand, but machine-stitching will make work go more quickly.

Use a one quarter-inch seam allowance, unless otherwise specified. Hand work should be done carefully so that the seams are strong. For machine-sewing, double-stitch or reinforce just inside the seam line with a zigzag row.

If you've never worked on tiny sewing projects, it might be a good idea to practice on a few pillows or floor cushions before trying some of the more elaborate furniture pieces in this chapter. The basic techniques are the same whether you're producing sofa or chair cushions, bolsters, mattresses, or simple accent pillows. All you have to do is stitch together a fabric bag, leaving one side open, turn right-side out, fill with stuffing, and hand sew the remaining side closed. Basic pillow directions follow.

ALL-PURPOSE PILLOW

All-purpose pillows can be used on beds or sofas and as attractive decorative accents (see figure 4).

MATERIALS NEEDED:

lightweight but durable fabric scraps — either cotton, cotton-polyester
    blends, or polyester double knit
old stockings or kapok for stuffing
thread

TOOLS NEEDED:

needle
sewing machine (optional)
scissors
ruler

PROCEDURE:

1. For each pillow, cut out a fabric rectangle 3 1/2 inches long and 2 inches wide.
2. Fold each piece of fabric in half, right sides together, to form a rectangle 2 inches long and 1 3/4 inches wide. Stitch the 1 3/4-inch sides closed, using a 1/4-inch seam. Leave the third side open for stuffing.

3. Turn pillow bag right-side out. Stuff lightly. Turn raw edges under and carefully hand stitch the opening closed.

LARGE FLOOR PILLOWS

The large floor pillow shown in figure 4 makes a nice addition to a modern dollhouse room. Materials needed and construction are exactly the same as for the all-purpose pillows described above, *except* that you must use a piece of fabric 6 1/2 inches long and 3 1/2 inches wide. Fold in half to form a rectangle 3 1/2 inches long and 3 1/4 inches wide.

BASIC BED

The bed pictured in figure 6 is very simple to make and can be used with several different headboards.

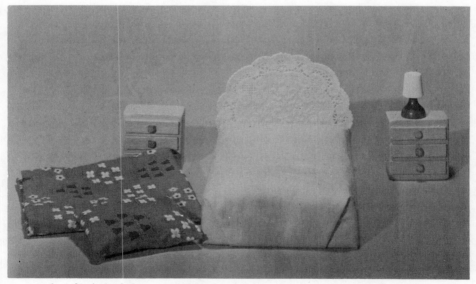

FIG. 6: *A basic bed shown with ornate headboard, nightstands, and linens.*

The basic form is a small cardboard box, padded and covered with fabric. The sturdiness of the box selected is important in this project. If the one you're using seems flimsy, reinforce it by wrapping all exterior surfaces with masking tape, for extra strength. The box will not show when the bed is finished, so you can also use a container that has been cut down to the size needed and taped back together.

Because dollhouse rooms tend to be small, the bed shown is proportionately shorter than a life-size counterpart. If you want one that's longer, simply choose a slightly larger box.

MATERIALS NEEDED:

a cardboard box, approximately 5 1/2 inches long, 3 1/2 inches wide, and 1 inch high
masking tape
muslin, percale, or other medium-weight fabric remnant for mattress cover
light padding, such as a discarded crib pad or receiving blanket
thread

TOOLS NEEDED:

scissors
ruler
white household glue

PROCEDURE:

1. To make a "mattress" for the bed, cut out several thicknesses of padding material the same size as the top of the bed. The layers should be about 1/4 inch thick.
2. Very lightly glue the padding layers together. Then glue them to the top surface of the box. Let dry.
3. Cut out a fabric rectangle 9 inches long and 7 inches wide. (If you are covering a longer box, cut out a larger rectangle.)
4. Wrap material over the top and sides of the box, folding ends down flat as if wrapping a package. Smooth excess fabric to the underside of the box and glue raw edges to bottom. Let dry.
5. Add pillows and bed linens as desired.

HIGH BED

For a "high" bed, complete the project just described. Then glue four 1/2-inch beads to the bottom corners of the box frame. Let dry.

ORNATE HEADBOARD FOR BASIC BED

This easy project, shown in figure 6, is made from paper doilies glued and sewn together and finished with several coats of spray varnish. The headboard is then glued and whip stitched to the bed frame. (See figure 7 for the bed and headboard in a room setting.)

FIG. 7: *A pleasant traditional bedroom.*

MATERIALS NEEDED:

ten paper doilies, each 4 inches in diameter
thread
white household glue
spray varnish

TOOLS NEEDED:

ruler
needle

PROCEDURE:

1. Very lightly glue ten paper doilies together. Let dry and take several small stitches through the holes in the lace pattern for additional strength.
2. Cover with two or three coats of spray varnish. Let dry.

3. Bend forward one edge of the headboard to a ninety-degree angle. This will form a small tab that will slip underneath the bed. The tab should be about 1/2 inch deep at its widest point.

4. Glue tab under bed and let dry. Then stitch the sides of the headboard to the fabric of the "mattress" with small whip stitches.

EASY LOUNGE-SLEEP SOFA

The seat of this simple sofa (shown in figure 8) is a foam-rubber rectangle covered with fabric. The back can be a fabric bolster stuffed with padding, or a set of three all-purpose pillows.

FIG. 8: Easy-to-make lounge-sleep sofa.

Any lightweight, durable cloth can be used for the sofa and bolster or pillow coverings, including cotton, acrylic, or polyester stretch knits. The sofa shown in figure 8 is covered with a medium-weight polyester double knit.

MATERIALS NEEDED FOR SEAT AND BOLSTER (OR PILLOW BACK):

medium-weight fabric remnant
polyurethane foam or foam-rubber piece, 1 inch thick
nylon stockings or kapok for stuffing
thread

TOOLS NEEDED:

scissors
ruler
needle

PROCEDURE FOR SEAT:

1. Cut out the following pieces:
two fabric rectangles 3 1/2 inches long and 2 inches wide
one fabric rectangle 8 1/2 inches long and 6 inches wide
one polyurethane-foam rectangle 5 inches long and 3 inches wide
2. Lay the larger fabric rectangle reverse side up on a flat work surface
and position the foam on the fabric. Firmly wrap the fabric around the
foam. Lap so that the seam will be on the edge of the unit. Turn under
the overlapping edge and stitch closed.
3. To finish the first end of the seat, fold the raw edges of the fabric
under until they are even with the edge of the foam rectangle. Cover
the exposed end of the foam rectangle with one of the smaller fabric
rectangles, working so that the right side of the fabric is exposed and
smoothing all raw edges to the inside. Neatly hand stitch into place.
Smooth out and finish second end of seat in the same way.

PROCEDURE FOR BOLSTER:

1. Cut out the following pieces:
two fabric circles 1 1/2 inches in diameter
one fabric rectangle 6 inches long and 3 3/4 inches wide
2. Fold the fabric rectangle, right sides together, to form a long strip.
Stitch a 1/4-inch seam along the 6-inch edge to form a tube from this
strip. Turn tube right-side out.
3. Stuff the bolster tube heavily with padding. Fold in about 1/2 inch
of fabric at each end of the tube. Using a needle and thread, sew the
first circle, right-side out, over the tube end. Tuck raw edges of the circle
under about 1/8 inch as you work, to form a smooth seam.
4. Check stuffing for smoothness, adding more as needed to remove any
wrinkles or lumpiness. Also check the length of the tube by comparing
it to the seat unit. Adjust open end of bolster by tucking in or pulling
out fabric slightly if necessary.
5. Sew on second circle, using same method as for first, to completely
close bolster.
    If pillows are desired for the back of the sofa instead of a bolster,
make three all-purpose pillows, as described earlier in this chapter.

LOOSE PILLOW SOFA

A loose-pillow sofa can be used in many decors, depending on the fabric and finishing details selected; for instance, the sofa shown on the left in figure 5 will look fine in a modern setting. As you can see from the sofa shown on the right in the photograph, the same basic piece with the addition of a skirted bottom fits into a more traditional room.

Construction of the basic design is fairly simple. The sofa frame is made from medium-weight cardboard, covered with material so that neither the cardboard nor the raw edges of the fabric shows.

The seat-back cushion unit is actually made from one piece of fabric. When stuffed and stitched, this cushion unit looks like four separate pillows.

Don't be deceived by the small size of the loose-pillow sofa when selecting fabric. To be sure you have enough, choose a remnant at least a half-yard long. Use lightweight but durable material. Stretchy or heavy fabric is not suitable.

Directions follow for the modern sofa. The one shown in figure 5 is covered with a cotton broadcloth. For finishing details of the traditional one, see the next project.

MATERIALS NEEDED:

medium-weight fabric remnant
discarded nylon stockings or kapok for stuffing
shoebox-weight cardboard
white household glue
three popsicle sticks for modern sofa base
thread

TOOLS NEEDED:

heavy-duty scissors
ruler
needle
sewing machine (optional)
tin snips
pencil

PROCEDURE:

1. Cut out and label the following pieces:
one cardboard rectangle 5 inches long and 3 inches wide for sofa seat-back frame

two cardboard rectangles 1 1/2 inches long and 1 inch wide for sofa arms
one fabric rectangle 7 inches long and 6 inches wide for sofa seat-back upholstery
two 2 1/2-inch fabric squares for arm upholstery
one fabric rectangle 6 1/2 inches long and 5 1/2 inches wide for sofa seat-back cushion unit
two fabric rectangles 3 1/2 inches long and 2 inches wide for arm bolsters

2. With a scissors point, score the seat-back-frame cardboard piece lightly across the middle and gently fold backward along this line as shown in figure 9.

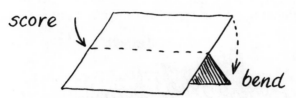

FIG. 9: Loose-pillow sofa-frame scoring directions.

3. Lay the seat-back upholstery piece right-side down on a flat work surface. Unfold the cardboard (with the inside of the crease facing you) and center it on the fabric. There should be more fabric overlap at the top and bottom of the cardboard than at the sides.
4. Put a line of glue on side and bottom edges of fabric (see figure 10).

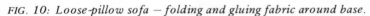

FIG. 10: Loose-pillow sofa — folding and gluing fabric around base.

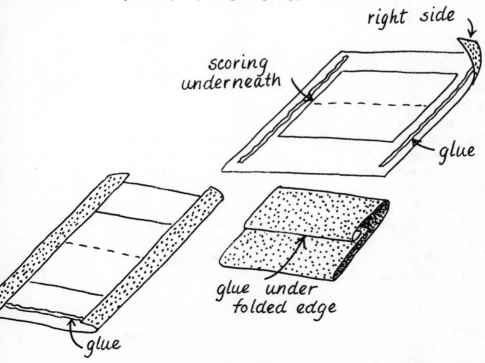

Fold over the two side edges and press against the cardboard frame piece. Then fold over bottom edge and press against cardboard.

5. Put a line of glue on the *right side* of the top edge of the fabric. Turn this glued edge under 1/4 inch and lap it over the bottom raw edge. This will completely encase the cardboard in upholstery, with no raw edges showing. Glue and pinch together the side edges of the fabric to form a smooth "seam." Rebend the fabric-covered frame back to a sitting position.

6. Arm pieces are covered in exactly the same way as the seat-back frame; except *do not* score cardboard pieces or bend them in the middle.

7. Glue bottom and back edges of upholstered arms to bottom and back of upholstered seat-back frame as shown in figure 11.

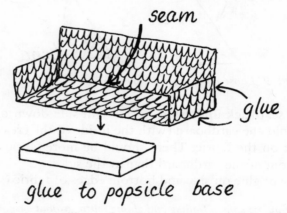

seam

glue

glue to popsicle base

FIG. 11: *Loose-pillow sofa —gluing on arms; putting on base.*

8. With the 6 1/2-inch-by-5 1/2-inch fabric rectangle already cut out, make the sofa cushion unit. Fold the fabric piece, right sides together, to form a rectangle 5 1/2 inches by 3 1/4 inches. Using a needle and thread or sewing machine, stitch the 3 1/4-inch-long sides 1/4 inch from each edge — this will form a fabric bag.

9. Turn bag right-side out. Stuff lightly. Then turn under raw fabric edge of the remaining side and carefully stitch the bag closed by hand.

10. To complete the cushion unit, take two lines of stitching across the middle of the cushion — one vertical and one horizontal — to divide the unit into four equal parts. The completed cushion unit will have the appearance of four separate cushions when placed on its sofa frame.

11. For arm bolsters, make two small pillows, using the 3 1/2-inch-by-2-inch fabric rectangles previously cut out. For each pillow, fold the fabric in half, right sides together, to form a rectangle 2 inches long and 1 3/4 inches wide. Stitch the 1 3/4-inch-long sides 1/4 inch from each

edge. Turn pillow right-side out, stuff, and close opening by hand. Tuck pillows in sofa corners.

12. For sofa base, cut rounded ends off three popsicle sticks with a tin snips. From one stick, cut two pieces, each 1 1/2 inches long; the two remaining sticks will each be 4 inches long.

13. Form a bottomless box with the four pieces and glue them together as shown in figure 11. Use a damp cloth to wipe away any excess glue on the outside of the base. Let dry. If desired, finish with paint or stain. The sofa base shown was finished with two coats of brown wax-based shoe polish. (For more information on wood finishes see chapter 4.)

14. Glue the base to the sofa bottom and let dry.

SKIRTED SOFA

This sofa, shown in figure 5, should be covered with medium-weight fabric in either a traditional print or solid color. Make the modern sofa just described, except omit the popsicle-stick base. Instead, glue four 1/2-inch beads to the corners of the sofa bottom to form legs. Then add a skirt, using the directions that follow. The sofa shown is covered with medium-weight cotton (see plate 2).

PROCEDURE FOR SOFA SKIRT:

1. Cut out an additional strip of sofa fabric 20 inches long and 1 1/4 inches wide.

2. To finish raw edges, turn under both long sides of the fabric 1/4 inch and stitch by hand or machine.

3. Run a gathering thread along one side. Pull up and adjust to the sofa bottom, allowing a 1/2-inch overlap at the back.

4. On the reverse side of the ruffle, put a line of white household glue along the gathered edge. With fingers, press this glued edge to the bottom of the sofa upholstery. Be sure the raw ends of the gathered skirt are at the sofa back and that the skirt hangs evenly.

5. Lap the raw ends, turning the top one under 1/4 inch. Glue and stitch flat.

LOOSE PILLOW CHAIR

Like the loose-pillow sofa just described, the loose-pillow chair shown in figure 12 can be used with a variety of decorating schemes.

31

FIG. 12: Comfortable and homey loose-pillow chair.

Upholstered with an Early American print and accented with a skirted bottom, the chair complements a traditional room. The same basic piece, made with a wood base instead of a skirt, can be used in a contemporary setting. For another look, use 1/2-inch beads for legs.

The loose-pillow chair, which is upholstered in a medium-weight cotton print, is put together in the same way as the traditional loose-pillow sofa described above. The cardboard seat-back and arm pieces are covered with fabric. Then a cushion unit, arms, and skirt are added.

MATERIALS NEEDED:

fabric remnant
discarded nylon stockings or kapok for stuffing
shoebox-weight cardboard
white household glue
four 1/2-inch beads for legs
thread

TOOLS NEEDED:

heavy-duty scissors
ruler
needle
sewing machine (optional)
pencil

PROCEDURE:

1. Cut and label the following pieces:

one cardboard rectangle 3 inches long and 2 1/4 inches wide for chair seat-back frame

two cardboard rectangles 1 1/2 inches long and 1 inch wide for chair arms

one fabric rectangle 6 1/2 inches long and 3 1/4 inches wide for chair seat-back upholstery

two fabric rectangles 2 1/2 inches square for arm upholstery

one fabric rectangle 6 1/2 inches long and 2 1/2 inches wide for chair seat-back cushion

two fabric rectangles 3 inches long and 1 3/4 inches wide for arm bolsters

one fabric strip 13 inches long and 1 1/4 inches wide for ruffle

2. Follow steps 2 through 7 in directions for modern loose-pillow sofa.

3. With the 6 1/2-inch-long and 2 1/2-inch-wide rectangle of fabric already cut out, make the chair cushion unit. Fold the fabric piece, right sides together, to form a rectangle 3 1/4 by 2 1/2 inches. Using a needle and thread or sewing machine, stitch the 3 1/4-inch-long sides 1/4 inch from each edge — this will form a fabric bag.

4. Turn bag right-side out. Stuff lightly. Then turn under raw fabric edge and carefully stitch bag closed by hand. To complete the cushion unit, take a line of stitching horizontally across the middle of the cushion — this will give it the appearance of two separate cushions when placed on the chair frame.

5. For arm bolsters, make two small pillows, using the 3-inch-by-1 3/4-inch fabric rectangles already cut out. For each pillow, fold the fabric in half to form a rectangle 1 1/2 inches wide and 1 3/4 inches long. Stitch the 1 1/2-inch-long sides 1/4 inch from each edge. Turn pillow right-side out; stuff and close opening by hand. Tuck pillows into chair corners.

6. Glue four 1/2-inch beads to the corners of the chair bottom for legs. Let dry.

7. Make the chair skirt with the strip of fabric 13 inches long and 1 1/4 inches wide already cut out. To finish the raw edges, turn up both long sides of the fabric 1/4 inch and stitch by hand or machine.

8. Run a gathering thread along one long side. Pull up and adjust to chair bottom; allow a 1/2-inch overlap at the back.

9. On reverse side of ruffle, put a line of white glue along the gathered edge. With fingers, press glued edge to bottom of chair upholstery. Be sure the raw ends of the gathered skirt are at the chair back and that the skirt hangs evenly.

10. Lap the raw ends, turning the top one under 1/4 inch. Glue and stitch flat.

For a modern version of the loose-pillow chair just described, omit the skirt and bead legs and add a wooden base made from two popsicle sticks. Cut the sticks to form four pieces — two of them 1 7/8 inches long and two of them 1 1/2 inches long. Form a bottomless box with the four pieces, bonding them together with white household glue. Use a damp cloth to wipe away any excess glue on the outside of the base. Let dry. If desired, finish with paint or stain. (For more information on wood finishes see chapter 4.) Glue the base to the chair bottom and let dry.

BUCKET CHAIR

This chair is easily constructed and can be adapted to several settings. With tailored trim, the piece is a modern living-room chair like the one in figure 13. With an ornate, metallic trim, it becomes a fancy boudoir chair.

FIG. 13: Modern bucket chair "upholstered" in felt and trimmed with knitting yarn.

The chair frame is a length of toilet-paper roll from which a U-shaped piece is cut. Both the inner and outer surfaces of the frame are covered with felt. Then the chair bottom is glued into place; stuffing is inserted in the base; and the felt seat is glued on top. The chair shown in figure 13 is covered with green felt and trimmed with matching knitting yarn.

MATERIALS NEEDED:

discarded toilet-paper roll
6-inch square of felt
tracing paper (or lightweight paper)
white household glue
discarded nylon stockings or kapok for stuffing
1/4 yard of wool or narrow metallic braid
shoebox-weight cardboard

TOOLS NEEDED:

pencil
scissors
ruler

PROCEDURE:

1.   Trace pattern pieces A, B, C, and D on paper and cut out. Label the pieces and transfer dotted cutting line shown to piece B (see figure 14).

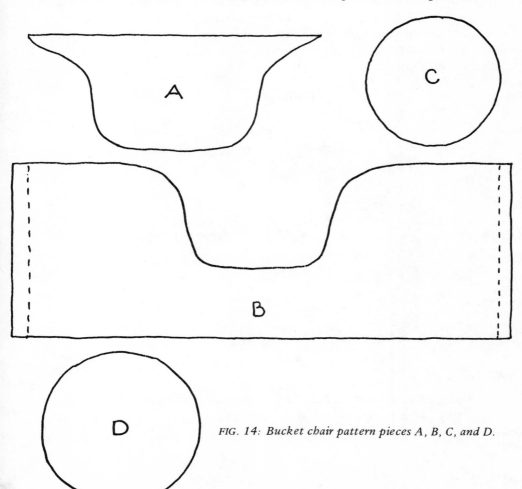

FIG. 14: Bucket chair pattern pieces A, B, C, and D.

2. Cut a section of toilet-paper roll 1 7/8 inches long.
3. Wrap pattern piece A around the roll, placing longest edge of piece A against the edge of the tube, as shown in figure 15. Trace around the

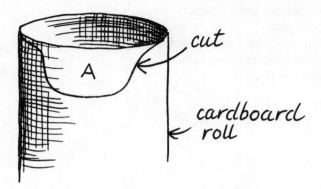

FIG. 15: *Bucket chair — tube with part cut away.*

pattern piece on the tube with a pencil. Cut away tube along this line.
4. Using pattern piece B, cut out two felt pieces; make the second one smaller, as indicated by using the dotted cutting line. The larger piece will go around the outside of the tube, and the smaller one around the inside (see figure 16).

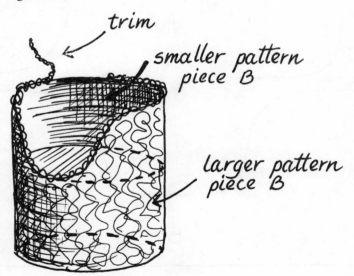

FIG. 16: *Bucket chair — gluing on trim.*

5. Using pattern piece C, cut one felt and one cardboard circle.
6. Using pattern piece D, cut one felt circle.

7. Apply a thin coat of glue to the outside of the tube. Fit the larger felt piece B around the roll, smoothing and pressing down. If necessary, trim felt with scissors to conform to the tube edges.

8. Put a coat of glue on the inside of the tube and cover with smaller felt piece B, the same way the outside piece was applied.

9. Center cardboard circle on larger felt circle and glue down. Then glue the two circles, felt side out, to tube bottom.

10. When chair is completely dry, fill seat base with stuffing. Tamp down with fingers. Cover stuffing with the smaller felt circle, smoothing and gluing into place.

11. To finish chair, apply a thin ribbon of glue to the exposed cardboard edge. Starting and ending at the top center back, as shown in figure 16, press down trim over edge. Smooth with fingers to achieve an even line.

CURVED BACK VICTORIAN STYLE SOFA

The curved-back sofa (see figure 1 and plate 3) is an elegant addition to a traditionally furnished dollhouse. Since the sofa is constructed primarily by sewing, rather than by gluing the pieces together, it will take more time and skill to make than most of the other projects in this chapter.

The sofa-back frame is a curved plastic piece; the seat frame is cardboard. Both are padded and covered with a dressy fabric such as velvet, velveteen, chintz, or lightweight, no-wale corduroy. (Red velvet was used for the sofa shown.) Arms are rolled strips of fabric glued into position. Sofa legs are decorative opaque beads glued to the bottom.

MATERIALS NEEDED:

fabric remnant
discarded plastic 1/2-gallon ice-cream container
shoebox-weight cardboard
discarded nylon stockings or kapok for stuffing
thread
four 1/2-inch opaque beads
white household glue

TOOLS NEEDED:

scissors
X-acto or razor-blade knife
needle
sewing machine (optional)

ball-point pen
fine-grit sandpaper
iron and ironing board
tracing or lightweight paper

PROCEDURE:

1. Trace the three pattern pieces A, B, and C on paper and cut out (see figures 17 and 18). Label the pattern pieces. Be sure to transfer the broken cutting line to pieces A and B.

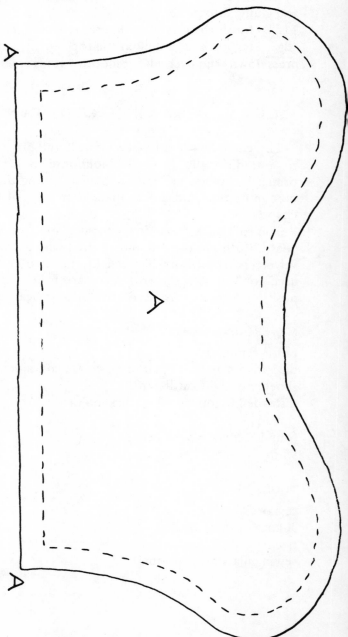

FIG. 17: Victorian sofa pattern piece A.

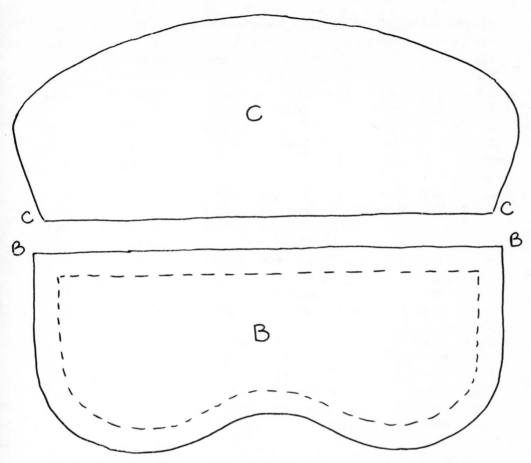

FIG. 18: *Victorian sofa pattern pieces B and C.*

2. Using the patterns just prepared, cut out the following construction pieces in fabric:

two sofa-back pieces, using the solid cutting line on pattern piece A
two sofa-seat pieces, using the solid cutting line on pattern piece B
one sofa-bottom piece, using pattern piece C

In addition, cut out two fabric rectangles 4 inches long and 1 3/4 inches wide for sofa arms. Set all fabric pieces aside.

3. Using the broken cutting line on pattern piece B, cut out a cardboard seat-frame piece.

4. Using the broken cutting line on pattern piece A, outline the sofa-back frame on the side of the plastic container in pen. Score the outline in the plastic, using an X-acto or razor-blade knife — this will take a firm hand, so go slowly; mistakes will show in the finished sofa. When the plastic frame piece is completely scored, cut through it with the blade. If the back-frame piece has any rough edges, carefully sand smooth.

5. The sofa-back upholstery is constructed like a pillow, into which the frame piece and stuffing are inserted. Leaving the straight, bottom edge open, and with right sides together, sew the two sofa-back fabric pieces together, using a 1/4-inch seam. Reinforce with a second line of stitching close to the first; use zigzag stitch, if possible. Trim excess fabric from seam at curves to about 1/8 inch.

6. Turn fabric right-side out and insert plastic frame. Fabric will curve to the line of the plastic; the inward curve is the sofa front. Using small amounts of stuffing, pad the sofa front until a soft, even appearance is achieved.

7. The sofa-seat fabric pieces are put together in exactly the same way as the sofa-back upholstery, described in step 5.

8. Turn the seat fabric right-side out and insert cardboard frame. Pad the "top" of the seat with stuffing until a plump, smooth line is achieved.

9. Lay the sofa-back and seat, with stuffed sides together, so that the raw edges are parallel. The sofa back and seat should be lying face to face. Using a needle and thread, stitch the two touching edges of the back and seat together with a 1/4-inch seam. The underside of the sofa seat and the outside of the sofa back will remain open. If the fabric of the sofa back is too slack, pull tight and adjust the seam as necessary. The seat and back fabric must fit snugly together.

10. Following the curve of the sofa bottom, stitch the remaining raw edge of the back and the curved edge of fabric bottom piece C, right sides together, using a 1/4-inch seam. Insert padding under the open side of bottom piece C as needed to form a flat, firm base (see figure 19).

11. Close the sofa bottom by turning the straight raw edge of bottom fabric piece C under 1/4 inch, overlapping it over the remaining raw edge of the sofa seat, and stitching closed by hand. When completed, the bottom will appear as shown in figure 20.

12. For sofa arms, lay the two small fabric rectangles, already cut out, right sides down on a work surface. Fold in the raw edges of the long sides 1/4 inch. Press down these folded edges with an iron.

13. Roll up each strip to form a tube-shaped bolster. Only one raw edge of each tube will show. With needle and thread, whip stitch over this raw edge to hold each bolster closed. Place a line of glue along this raw edge and on the end of each arm bolster. Press the bolsters to the seat and back of sofa. Let dry.

14. For legs, glue beads in position on underside of sofa. Let dry.

FIG. 20: Victorian sofa — bottom finished.

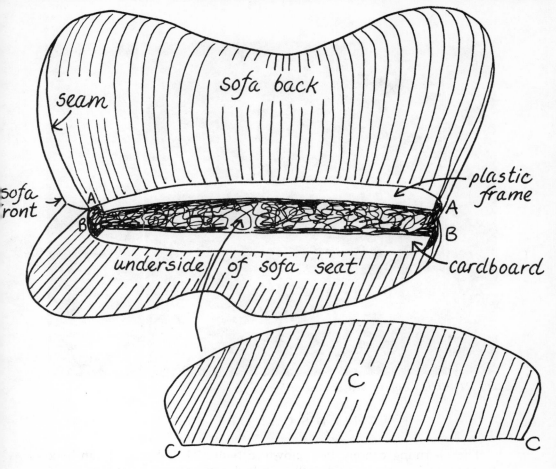

seam

sofa back

sofa front

plastic frame

A
B

A
B

underside of sofa seat

cardboard

C

C   C

FIG. 19: Victorian sofa — sewing sofa bottom together.

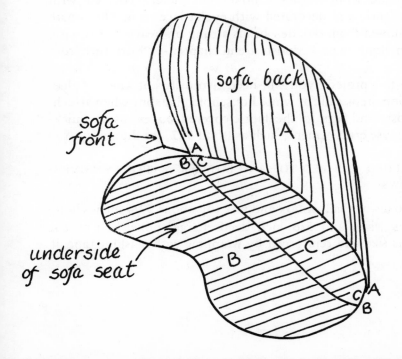

sofa back

A

sofa front

A
B C

underside of sofa seat

B   C

C A
B

FIG. 21: Child's canopy bed, shown with coverlet removed.

CHILD'S CANOPY BED

The charming canopy bed shown in figure 21 and plate 4 can be a focal point in a traditional dollhouse bedroom. The top and bottom of the bed are made from "lidless" boxes completely covered with medium-weight fabric and decorated with eyelet lace trim. The ornate posters are fashioned from wooden beads strung on heavy florist wire. Directions for making these bedposts are in chapter 4, "Furniture from Wood."

To complete this project, you will need two different kinds of glue. Most construction steps call for white household glue; but when attaching the bed posts and legs to the fabric-covered boxes, use a quick-drying multipurpose craft cement, such as Bond 527, for durability.

MATERIALS NEEDED FOR BED TOP AND BOTTOM, MATTRESS, COVER-LET, AND PILLOWS:

two "lidless" boxes or shallow box and box top about 5 1/4 inches long, 3 3/4 inches wide, and 5/8 inch deep. Larger boxes can be cut down to this size and reinforced by wrapping with masking tape, if necessary.)

1 1/4 yards of eyelet lace trim, about 1 1/2 inch wide
1/2 yard of eyelet lace trim about 3/4 inch wide
medium-weight fabric remnant for bed top, bottom, coverlet, and
    pillows
muslin or other medium-weight remnant for mattress
nylon stockings or kapok for stuffing
thread
white household glue
multipurpose craft cement

TOOLS NEEDED:

scissors
ruler
iron and ironing board
needle
sewing machine (optional)
   Directions follow for the bed shown in figure 21. If a larger bed is
desired, dimensions for fabric and eyelet lace will change proportionally.

PROCEDURE:

1. Make bedposts as directed in chapter 4. Set aside.
2. To cover the canopy, cut two rectangles of fabric. The larger, which
will cover the top and sides, should be about 10 1/2 inches long and 8
inches wide. The smaller piece, which will cover the inside bottom of
the canopy, should be 5 3/4 inches long and 4 1/4 inches wide.
3. Turn under the raw edges of the small fabric rectangle 1/4 inch on
all four sides and press flat with an iron. Set aside. Lay the larger fabric
rectangle right-side down on a work surface. Lightly coat the reverse
side of the fabric with glue. Then attach the fabric to the box, pulling
the raw edges to the inside so that the entire surface of the box, except
for the inside bottom, is completely enclosed in fabric (see figure 22).
4. To hide the raw edges and to finish the underside of the canopy,
glue the smaller fabric rectangle to the inside bottom of the lid. Be sure
the fabric is right-side out. Let dry. Canopy is now completed.
5. To finish the lower frame of the bed, repeat steps 2, 3, and 4, using
the second box.
6. To join the top and bottom of the bed, poke a small hole in the
four corners of each covered box with a scissors point. Thread protruding wire ends of bedposts through these holes.
7. To finish tops of posts, use craft cement to glue four additional
beads over the protruding wires. Let dry. Turn over bed and repeat procedure to make bed legs. Let dry. For additional stability, put some

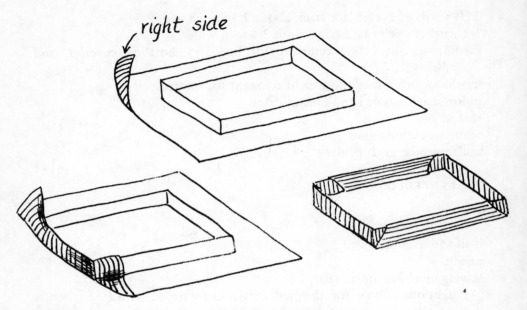

right side

FIG 22: Canopy bed — instructions for gluing and wrapping boxes.

extra craft cement where the top and bottom of each bedpost touches the inside of the covered boxes. Let dry.

8. Using white glue, attach 1 1/2-inch-wide eyelet lace trim around the bed top and bottom for ruffle, as shown in figure 21. Overlap the lace at one corner. Fold under the raw edge of the top piece; stitch and glue down. Let dry.

9. For mattress, cut out a rectangle of muslin 10 1/2 inches long and 4 inches wide. Fold the muslin in half to form a bag 5 1/4 inches long and 4 inches wide. Stitch the long sides of the bag closed and turn right-side out. Stuff fairly heavily; turn in remaining raw edges and stitch closed by hand.

10. For pillows, make two all-purpose pillows, described near the beginning of this chapter.

11. To make coverlet, cut out a piece of fabric 6 inches long and 4 1/4 inches wide. Make a narrow hem on all four edges — either by hand or machine. Then stitch a border of 3/4-inch eyelet lace trim to the sides and bottom. Omit lace at head of coverlet. Be sure to turn under raw edges at ends of lace strip.

FIG. 23: This cozy room features a chest, two tables, a chair, and an étagère — all made from wood.

4

Furniture from Wood

You don't have to be a carpenter to make a wide assortment of doll-house furniture from wood. Instead, work with precut pieces — such as children's blocks, spools, popsicle sticks, and wooden beads. Another possibility is balsa wood, which can be purchased in hobby shops and cut to the desired size by using an X-acto or razor-blade knife, rather than a saw.

With these basic materials, you can easily create chests, tables, benches, canopy bedposts, and even chairs, in a variety of attractive styles. Some examples can be seen in figure 23.

Although wooden beads can be purchased already stained and varnished, the other wood-construction materials described in this chapter come unfinished. You can either leave them natural for the soft look of birch or oak, or finish them using several different techniques. Scratch-covering furniture polish (not ordinary furniture polish), wax-based shoe polish, stain and varnish, spray enamel, acrylic paint, decoupage finish, latex paint, and even metallic wax rub may be suitable — it all depends on the specific project involved.

With any of these finishes, you must test a scrap piece of wood or the back of the constructed item to be sure of getting exactly the result or tone you want. The photographs in this chapter show many of the looks that can be achieved with different finishing processes.

Scratch-covering furniture polish: Rub one or two coats on the wood surface, using a soft cloth. Excess polish must be wiped off several times or the surface will remain sticky.

Wax-based shoe polish: Apply one or two coats with a soft cloth. For hard-to-reach corners, use a cotton swab. Wax-based shoe polish can be applied over or under scratch-covering furniture polish to enrich or change the tone of the finish.

Stain and varnish: Follow the manufacturer's directions.

Spray enamel: Use in a well-ventilated area. If working indoors, place the furniture piece being sprayed inside a cardboard box to contain the fumes. Two or more coats of spray enamel are needed for wood. Let dry thoroughly between coats.

Acrylic paint: For a matte finish, apply at least two coats with a small brush.

Spray varnish or decoupage finish: This clear finish, sold for use in craft or decoupage projects, can be applied over raw wood and acrylic or latex paint to add gloss and protection to surfaces.

Latex wall paint: Latex paint can give either a flat or semigloss finish. Apply at least two coats to furniture pieces. Don't brush on paint too heavily, and let one coat dry thoroughly before adding another.

Metallic wax rub: A deep-toned metallic wax rub will add a rich luster when applied over furniture stain and an antique look when used over paint. Follow manufacturer's directions.

Gluing

If the project you're completing involves bonding wood to wood, an extra-strong, water-soluble glue — such as Titebond (sold in hobby shops for airplane model building) — will give good results. With a damp cloth, carefully wipe away any glue that seeps out during construction — this will make your workmanship appear neater, but it will also ensure that a finish can be applied more readily to the wood.

In some of the following projects, directions specify that, for proper bonding, a multipurpose craft cement such as Bond 527 should be used. Since this glue is *not* water soluble and cannot be completely wiped away as you work, it will prevent stain and wax-based shoe polish from adhering evenly to the wood. Therefore, it should be applied very sparingly to avoid unnecessary seepage. Any drips on the wood surface must be sanded away completely before a stain or shoe-polish finish is applied. Paint can be applied without sanding.

Wood Blocks

Wood blocks are a good base for sturdy dressers, night tables, and other standing pieces. Although the items do not have drawers that actually open, they are quite realistic looking and are very easy to make.

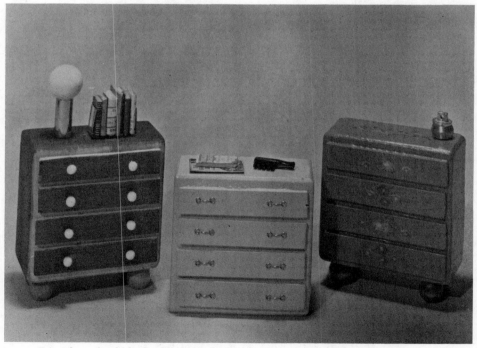

FIG. 24: *Three bachelor's chests made from three identical blocks of wood. Notice how different looks have been achieved by varying finishing and decorating details.*

FIG. 25: Night table, modern armoire, and storage units. These simple pieces, created from children's blocks, can be finished or left natural.

The pieces shown in figures 24 and 25 were created with children's building blocks. If you don't have a discarded set on hand, look for blocks at garage sales. Other sources of suitable wood blocks are scraps from construction projects and lumberyards and packaged wood scraps sold in some craft and variety stores. Unpainted blocks work best; but finished ones can either be sanded down or repainted with good results.

Since real chests and standing units come in a variety of sizes and shapes, it is not necessary to find wood pieces that are identical to those used in the projects that follow. You can substitute blocks with similar dimensions and achieve the same general look.

Of the finishing processes described on the preceding pages, scratch-covering furniture polish, spray enamel, acrylic or latex paint, and clear decoupage or other varnish are recommended for furniture pieces made from wood blocks.

BACHELOR'S CHEST

With one simple block of wood, it is possible to produce several very distinctive styles of chests. The basic design of the three shown in figure 24 is the same; but by applying different finishes, legs, drawer pulls, and other details, three unique effects have been created. The chest shown on the left in figure 24 was finished with scratch-covering furniture polish, applied to the drawer fronts, sides, and top only. Small white beads were used for drawer pulls. The chest in the middle was sprayed with yellow enamel. Eyes from a hook-and-eye set are the drawer pulls. The chest on the right was covered with two coats of blue acrylic paint, decorated with flowers cut from a magazine, and finished with two coats of spray varnish.

To produce the basic bachelor's chest, you just glue four balsa wood strips to the wood block. The balsa strips can either be painted or stained first in a contrasting color, or glued on and then finished with the rest of the unit.

MATERIALS NEEDED:

a wood block, approximately 2 3/4 inches square and 1 3/4 inches thick
a 12-inch-long strip of 1/2-inch-wide and 1/8-inch-thick balsa wood
extra-strong water-soluble glue
desired finishing materials
8 tiny beads or eyes from hook-and-eye sets for drawer pulls (optional)

TOOLS NEEDED:

ruler
X-acto or razor-blade knife and supply of blades
fine-grit sandpaper

PROCEDURE:

1. Lightly sand the wooden block with fine-grit sandpaper to remove any soil or scratches and to prepare the surface for finishing. Be sure to smooth any rough edges.
2. Using an X-acto or razor-blade knife, cut four lengths from the balsa-wood strip. These should be 1/4 inch shorter than the width of the block being used. For a smooth cut, place the balsa wood on a flat work surface and press firmly through the front of the strip. Use the front of the cut lengths for the drawer fronts, since these edges will be neater.
3. Lay the block on its back. Place a thin line of glue on the back of all the balsa strips and, using figure 24 as a guide, arrange them on the block to suggest drawers. Weight down balsa pieces with a book or block for a few minutes. Remove weight and carefully wipe away any

excess glue that has oozed out. Replace weight and let chest dry.

4. Finish chest as desired. Glue on legs and hardware if you like.

NIGHTSTAND

This can be constructed in exactly the same way as the bachelor's chest, except that a smaller block is needed. For the nightstand shown in figure 25, a block 1 3/4 inches square and 3/4 inch thick was used. It was trimmed with three balsa strips, each 1 1/2 inches long, 3/8 inch wide, and 1/16 inch thick. Then the piece was covered with two coats of pale green latex paint and lightly sprayed with a coat of clear decoupage finish. Small wooden beads were cut in half with a pair of tin snips and glued on for drawer pulls.

STORAGE UNITS

Storage units suitable for a child's bedroom, a den, or other informal dollhouse settings can be created using the basic approach already described for the bachelor's chest. The units shown in figure 25 were each made by using a block 3 1/2 inches long, 1 3/4 inches high, and 7/8 inch thick.

The effect of two narrow drawers at the top and a wider one at the bottom was produced by using two pieces of balsa wood 3 5/16 inches long, 3/8 inch wide, and 1/8 inch thick, with an additional piece of balsa 3 5/16 inches long, 1/2 inch wide, and 1/8 inch thick.

The storage units shown in figure 25 were left natural.

MODERN ARMOIRE

A modern armoire is another piece that can be made from a block trimmed with balsa-wood strips. (Refer to *bachelor's chest* project for general instructions.) The unit shown in figure 25 was constructed from a block 5 1/2 inches high, 2 3/4 inches wide, and 1 3/8 inches thick.

Two balsa pieces 2 1/2 inches long, 1/2-inch wide, and 1/8-inch thick were added for the drawers. A third piece, 3 7/8 inches long, 1/8 inch wide, and 1/8 inch thick, was placed vertically down the middle of the block to suggest doors.

The armoire shown was covered with two coats of latex wall paint. A light application of clear decoupage finish was then sprayed over the paint. Finally, small oblong beads were glued on the unit for door and drawer handles.

SIDE-BY-SIDE REFRIGERATOR

The large block used to make the modern armoire could also serve as a side-by-side refrigerator. To make this appliance, omit the bottom drawers from the armoire and extend the dividing strip all the way down the center of the appliance. Cover with two or three coats of white enamel paint or with a color to match your dollhouse kitchen. Refrigerator and freezer handles can be made from ball-point-pen clips. Carefully pry off the clips. Cut away the tiny prongs at the end with tin snips, and glue the clips to the appliance front, rounded ends down, where the bead door handles are located on the armoire (figure 25).

Wood Spools

A simple, round table is easy to make by using a wood spool for a base and a variety of cast-off materials — a round of cardboard covered with self-adhesive paper, an old coaster, or a discarded plastic bottle or jar lid — on top.

Spools can be painted, stained, varnished, rubbed with wax-based shoe polish, or left natural.

SMALL TABLES

These can serve as coffee or end tables or as decorative plant stands (see figure 26). The look will vary depending on the thickness and diameter of the top selected. The tops for the low tables shown in figure 26 were made from a plastic medicine-bottle cap, and cardboard covered with self-adhesive paper.

MATERIALS NEEDED FOR ONE TABLE:

a wooden spool approximately 1 1/4 inches high
a cardboard circle or other suitable round, approximately 1 1/4 to 3 inches in diameter
multipurpose craft cement
self-adhesive paper and metallic-coated string if a cardboard round is being covered
desired finishing material for spool

51

FIG. 26: Dinette table and low tables with spool bases.

TOOLS NEEDED:

scissors (if a cardboard round is used)

PROCEDURE:

1. Finish table base as desired.
2. If a plastic top is being used, simply center it on the spool and glue down. This is easier if the table is put together upside down with the top on a flat work surface.
3. If a cardboard round is being used, cover the top surface with self-adhesive paper. For a finished look, glue metallic trim around the edge of the top to hide the raw edge. Then glue table top to base.

HIGH TABLES

These can be used as kitchen, small dining room, or patio tables, depending on the top size and what it's made from. The high table shown in figure 26 was produced from spools finished with wax-based shoe polish. The top is a cork coaster.

MATERIALS NEEDED FOR ONE TABLE:

two wooden spools, each about 1 1/4 inches high
one lightweight but sturdy coaster, heavy plastic top, or other round
    between 2 3/4 and 3 1/2 inches in diameter
multipurpose craft cement
desired finishing material for spools

PROCEDURE:

1. Finish the spools as desired.
2. Glue the two spools together and let dry.
3. Center the table top on the spool base and glue into place. This is easier to do if the table is put together upside down with the top resting on a flat work surface.

P o p s i c l e   S t i c k s

There are two very different looks that can be produced by using these small wooden sticks: to create "butcher block" furniture, work so that the narrow edge of the stick becomes the finished furniture surface; to give the look of boards, work so that the wide edge of the stick becomes the finished surface.

Although popsicle sticks that have been saved can be used in the following projects, you may want to purchase a package of sticks from a hobby or craft store. Not only will this provide you with a plentiful supply, but it will also ensure that your building materials are completely free from stickiness and discoloration.

You will need a pair of inexpensive tin snips for cutting popsicle sticks. Finishes that can be used include paint, furniture stain, and clear varnish or decoupage finish.

B U T C H E R   B L O C K   B E N C H

The bench pictured in figure 27 can be used as a coffee table, beside a couch, or for seating. Left natural, as shown, or varnished, it will have the butcher-block look; however, it can be finished with a dark stain or painted, if you wish.

The top of the bench is made by gluing popsicle sticks, flat sides together. Stick pieces are then added for legs.

MATERIALS NEEDED:

sixteen popsicle sticks

FIG. 27: *Dining table and bench made from popsicle sticks. Left natural, the bench has the look of butcher-block furniture.*

multipurpose craft cement
desired finishing material (optional)

TOOLS NEEDED:

tin snips
ruler
fine-grit sandpaper (necessary if a dark stain finish is used)

PROCEDURE:

1. On a flat work surface, glue fourteen popsicle sticks together along the wide edges. Work as neatly as possible, placing a thin line of glue on each stick. To make sure the bench top will be even, hold the sticks firmly against the flat surface as you glue. Carefully wipe away any drips. If glue oozes out as the sticks dry, turn over the unit so that the cleaner side becomes the top.

2. For bench legs, cut two popsicle sticks into 3/4-inch sections; you need eight sections with straight ends. For each leg, glue two sections, flat sides together, to form a double thickness. When dry, glue to the underside of the bench about 1/2 inch from the corners. If necessary, prop up the legs while they dry.

54

3. Add finish to bench as desired. If a dark stain is to be applied, carefully sandpaper away all traces of excess glue first, as it will interfere with absorption of the finish.

DINING TABLE

The construction method for this table (shown in figure 27) is exactly the same as for the bench just described, except that thirty-six sticks are needed for the top and eight 2 1/4-inch lengths are required for the legs. The table shown was finished with an application of dark furniture stain, accented with a metallic wax rub.

PICNIC TABLE

Although the table shown in figure 28 may look complicated to construct, it's actually a fairly simple project put together from sticks instead of boards; however, you must be sure the glue is thoroughly dry at each stage before proceeding to the next.

FIG. 28: Picnic table fashioned from popsicle-stick "boards."

First, the tabletop is made by gluing popsicle sticks on two parallel crosspieces. Then, **V**-shaped legs are braced against the crosspieces. Finally, bench supports and attached bench seats are glued into place.

The table pictured was finished with a dark wood stain.

MATERIALS NEEDED:

twenty-four popsicle sticks
multipurpose craft cement
desired finishing materials

TOOLS NEEDED:

tin snips
ruler
fine-grit sandpaper (necessary if a stain finish is desired)

PROCEDURE:

1. To make the tabletop, lay eight popsicle sticks flat sides down on a work surface. You will be fastening these sticks together with two additional sticks, which have each been cut with tin snips to a length of 3 inches.
2. Glue the two fastening sticks across the other sticks, about 1 1/4 inches from the scalloped edges, as shown in figure 29.

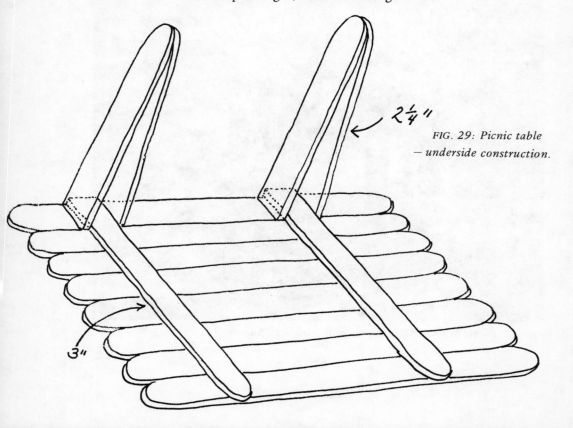

2¼"

FIG. 29: Picnic table
— underside construction.

3"

3. Table legs are made from eight popsicle sticks, each cut with tin snips to a length of 2 1/4 inches. Leave one end of each stick rounded.

4. To attach legs, lay the top of the table on its back on a work surface. In pairs, glue the cut ends of the legs to either side of the fastening sticks, as shown in figure 29. Let dry.

5. Working at the scalloped ends of the table, approximately 1 inch from the base of the legs, glue one popsicle stick across each pair of legs, as shown in figure 30. These two sticks are the supports on which the

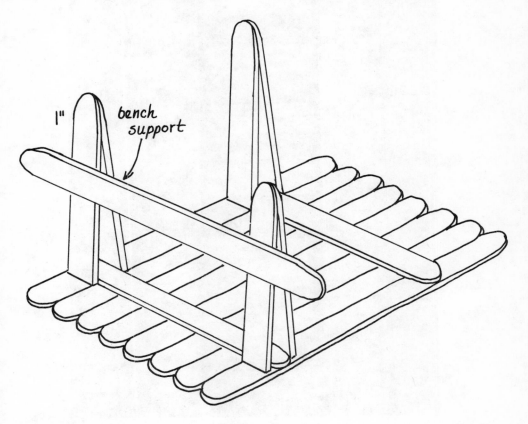

FIG. 30: Picnic table — attaching bench supports.

attached benches will rest. Let glue dry.

6. For attached bench seats, glue two sticks, flat sides resting across each end of the supports. Use figure 28 as a guide.

7. Finish picnic table as desired. If a furniture stain is to be applied, carefully sandpaper away all traces of excess glue first, as it will interfere with absorption of the finish.

A ladder-back chair is a charming addition to any dollhouse. Depending on the look you want, the piece can be left natural, painted, or finished with a clear varnish. Pictured in plate 2 and in figure 31, the chair is not

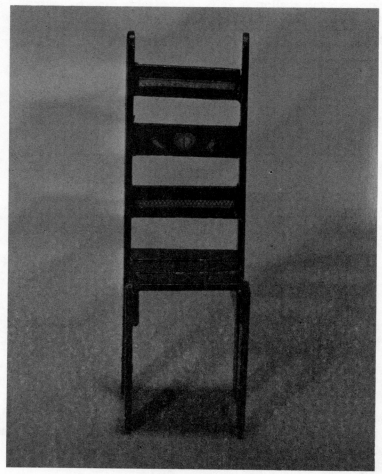

FIG. 31: Ladder-back chair shown with "country" finish.

really hard to make, but instructions must be followed carefully. Construction is completed in several steps: first, the two sides of the chair are formed; next, the seat slats are glued into place; and, finally, the back "ladders" are added. The key to success is in letting the pieces dry *completely* between these steps.

The chair shown was first covered with two coats of black acrylic paint. It was then decorated with colorful accent designs cut from magazines and glued to the "ladders." Last, two coats of clear decoupage finish were sprayed on top.

MATERIALS NEEDED FOR ONE CHAIR:

seven popsicle sticks
multipurpose craft cement
desired finishing material

TOOLS NEEDED:

tin snips
ruler

PROCEDURE:

1. Cut popsicle sticks to the following lengths, using tin snips:
using four sticks, cut eight pieces, each 1 1/4 inches long without any rounded ends
using one stick, cut two pieces, 1 3/4 inches long with one end of each piece left rounded
leave two sticks uncut

2. To form one side of the chair, assemble one full-length stick, a 1 3/4-inch piece, and a 1 1/4-inch piece. Glue these three together in the form of an h, *exactly* as shown in figure 32. Be sure the rounded end of the 1 3/4-inch piece is at the bottom right of the h.

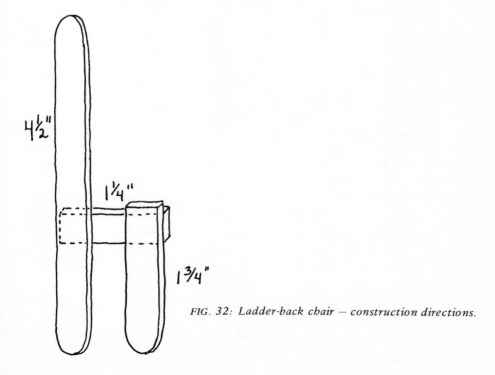

FIG. 32: Ladder-back chair — construction directions.

3. To form the other side of the chair, repeat the process, using three more stick pieces of the same sizes — *except* form a backwards **h**. Let the two sides of the chair dry thoroughly.

4. Holding the sides upright, place a thin line of glue on the top edge of the horizontal part of each **h** and allow to become tacky. Using figure 33

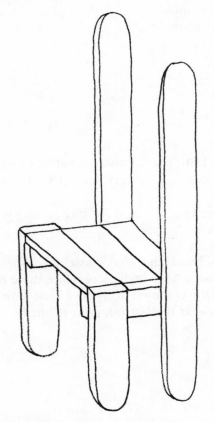

FIG. 33: Ladder-back chair — adding the seat slats.

as a guide, place three of the 1 1/4-inch pieces across the two sides, forming the chair seat. Prop up the chair carefully between bookends or blocks until completely dry.

5. Tip the chair so that its back is resting on a flat work surface. Put a thin line of glue on each *end* of the remaining 1 1/4-inch pieces and, starting from the bottom of the back, add the "ladders" to the chair, about 1/4 inch apart. If the "ladders" appear to be slipping out of place, gently squeeze the sides of the chair together until glue begins to set. Let dry.

6. Finish with paint or a clear varnish, if desired.

Balsa Wood

Balsa wood, available in hobby and craft shops, can be cut and used for tabletops, shelves, headboards, and cabinets. The wood comes in a variety of widths and thicknesses but is generally sold in three-foot-long strips.

For smooth cutting, be sure to use a sharp X-acto or razor-blade knife and change blades frequently.

Depending on the specific project, balsa can be finished with furniture stain, wax-based shoe polish, paint, or scratch-covering furniture polish.

COFFEE TABLE

The coffee table in figure 34 is just one of several that could be created using balsa wood for a top and beads for legs. Make the piece shown, using the directions that follow, or adapt the instructions to your own design.

FIG. 34: A traditional coffee table with bead legs.

The top of the table pictured was finished with an application of wax-based shoe polish.

61

MATERIALS NEEDED:

a balsa-wood strip 2 inches wide, 1/8 inch thick, and at least 4 inches
   long
eight macrame or other beads, approximately 1/2 inch high
small wooden dowels or toothpicks to fit bead holes
multipurpose craft cement
desired finishing material

TOOLS NEEDED:

X-acto or razor-blade knife and supply of blades
tin snips
ruler
fine-grit sandpaper

PROCEDURE:

1. With an X-acto or razor-blade knife, cut off a 4-inch-long section of
balsa wood.
2. Gently sand the edges of this wood piece at an angle to produce the
effect of a beveled edge. Also round the four corners of the tabletop
with sandpaper.
3. Apply desired finish to the top. Let dry.
4. Cut four 1-inch dowel or toothpick sections with tin snips.
5. To make each leg, string a pair of beads on a dowel. Carefully secure
beads to one another and to the dowel with glue. Let dry.
6. With tabletop flat on a work surface, glue the four bead legs to the
corners. Let dry.

HEADBOARD

A 1/8-inch-thick strip of balsa wood can also serve as a modern headboard. Cut a piece from the strip approximately 3 inches high and the
width of the bed. Finish the headboard, following directions 2 and 3 of
the coffee-table project just described. Glue to the bed with multipurpose craft cement.

BUFFET

A buffet is another attractive piece that can be fashioned from strips
of balsa wood.

Directions for the unit shown in figure 35 follow, but you can adapt

FIG. 35: Modern buffet made from pieces of balsa wood.

the procedure to your own requirements; for instance, the cabinet featured does not have a back, but one could be added for a free-standing unit.

To construct the buffet, first glue three accent pieces on the front to suggest doors. Then glue the front and sides together. Last, add the top of the unit.

The buffet shown was finished with a coat of scratch-covering furniture polish, followed by two coats of brown waxed-based shoe polish. (Shoe polish cannot be used alone in this project.) To achieve an attractive appearance using these finishes or a furniture stain, you must first sandpaper away all excess glue. Paint can be applied over traces of glue.

MATERIALS NEEDED:

a strip of balsa wood 2 1/2 inches wide, 1/8 inch thick, and 15 inches long
a strip of balsa wood 2 inches wide, 1/8 inch thick, and 6 inches long
multipurpose craft cement
desired finishing material

TOOLS NEEDED:

X-acto or razor-blade knife and supply of blades
ruler
pencil
fine-grit sandpaper

PROCEDURE:

1. From the wider balsa strip, cut out the following:
one rectangle 5 1/2 inches long and 2 1/2 inches wide for buffet front
one rectangle 5 1/2 inches long and 1 1/2 inches wide for buffet top
two rectangles 1 1/2 inches long and 2 1/2 inches wide for buffet sides
   From the narrower balsa strip, cut the following:
three rectangles 1 1/2 inches long and 2 inches wide for front door accents
2. Smooth edges of all pieces with sandpaper.
3. With buffet front face up on a flat work surface, center and glue on the three cabinet door accents as shown in figure 35. Apply glue sparingly to reduce drips and seepage. Weight down the door accents with a book and let dry.
4. Stand up the front and glue the two 1 1/2-inch-wide and 2 1/2-inch-high pieces at right angles to the front, forming the buffet sides. Prop up between blocks and let dry.
5. With a very thin line of glue, attach the top to the buffet base. For a good bond, weight down with a book while glue sets.
6. Finish as desired. If wood stain or scratch-covering furniture polish is to be used, completely sand away excess glue first.

KITCHEN BASE UNIT

Few dollhouses have a modern-looking kitchen, but if you're willing to spend a little time, you can create realistic cabinetry for this important room.

Make the 7-inch-long unit exactly as shown in figure 36, or modify it to custom fit any dollhouse dimensions. Just remember to leave room for a stove and refrigerator when planning your kitchen layout. (Directions for these appliances, as well as kitchen wall cabinets, are found in chapters 5 and 6.)

Although there are many construction pieces, the kitchen-base unit is made in several easy-to-follow steps. First the countertop is constructed; the sink is inserted; and faucet hardware is attached. Then realistic drawer and door details are glued to the base-unit front. Next, the sides

FIG. 36: Realistic-looking kitchen base unit fashioned from balsa wood. Note the hand cream pump spout used as a spigot.

are joined to the front. Finally, the countertop and cabinet unit are glued together.

The countertop of the unit pictured was covered with heavy, white self-adhesive paper. The cabinet unit was finished with two coats of yellow enamel paint. Furniture stain and shoe-polish finishes are not recommended for this project.

MATERIALS NEEDED:

a balsa-wood strip 12 inches long, 3 inches wide, and 1/8 inch thick for kitchen-base unit front and sides

a balsa-wood strip 12 inches long, 2 inches wide, and 1/8 inch thick for base-unit door and drawer pieces

a balsa-wood strip 12 inches long, 1/8 inch wide, and 1/8 inch thick for base-unit vertical accent strips (optional)

shoebox-weight cardboard

one discarded plastic or cardboard box or boxtop, approximately 2 inches long and 1 inch wide for sink. (A discarded Wilkinson single-edge razor-blade dispenser was used for the sink in figure 36.)

heavy opaque self-adhesive paper for countertop

small washer or nut for drain hole

pump spout from a small hand-cream (or similar) dispenser for spigot-
flow control
multipurpose craft cement
masking tape
six tiny beads for door and drawer pulls (optional)
enamel or semigloss latex paint

TOOLS NEEDED:

X-acto or razor-blade knife and supply of blades
ruler
pencil
scissors
fine-grit sandpaper

PROCEDURE:

1. To make the countertop, cut out a rectangle of cardboard 7 inches
long and 2 1/4 inches wide. Cut out a piece of self-adhesive paper 9
inches by 4 inches.
2. Cover the cardboard with the paper, neatly folding the paper under
on all sides.
3. To make a hole for the sink, on the wrong side of this countertop,
center the box that will be used. Trace around the box with a pencil.
Using the X-acto or razor-blade knife, cut through the top, working just
inside the penciled outline.
4. Turn the countertop to the right side and push the sink into place.
If the hole is too small, enlarge the cut slightly until the sink fits. Glue
into place and add strips of masking tape underneath for added support.
5. With a scissors point, punch a small hole in the countertop immediately behind the sink for the faucet-flow control. Insert the pump
spout and glue into place. Glue a nut into the center of the sink bottom
for a drain hole. Let dry.
6. To make the base-unit bottom, cut out the following pieces from
balsa wood with the X-acto or razor-blade knife:
from the 3-inch-wide strip, a piece 7 inches long and 3 inches wide for
    base-unit front
from the 3-inch-wide strip, 2 pieces 2 1/4 inches long and 3 inches high
    for base-unit sides
from the 2-inch-wide strip, three pieces 2 inches high and 1 1/2 inches
    wide for base-unit doors
from the 2-inch-wide strip, three pieces 1/2 inch high and 1 1/2 inches
    wide for base-unit drawers
from the 1/8-inch-wide strip, two pieces 3 inches long for base-unit
    accents

Sand smooth any rough edges and set aside.

7. With scissors, cut out two 3-inch squares of cardboard for base-unit interior supports. Set aside.

8. To complete the base-unit front, lay the 7-inch-long balsa rectangle on a flat work surface. Using figure 36 as a guide, glue the three door pieces, the three drawer pieces, and the two accent strips to the base-unit front. Carefully place a weight, such as a book, on top to ensure a good bond. Let pieces dry.

9. Fold the cardboard support squares in half and attach them to the back of the base-unit front with masking tape, as shown in figure 37.

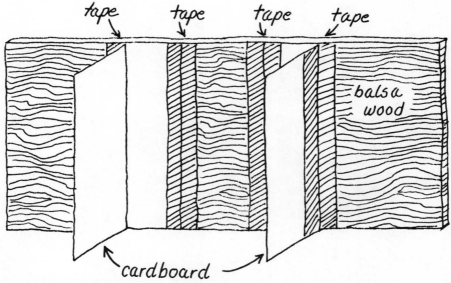

FIG. 37: Kitchen base unit — adding interior supports.

The front of the unit will now stand up.

10. Glue the 3-inch-by-2 1/4-inch balsa pieces at right angles to the base-unit front to form sides. Prop up the unit with blocks or bookends and let dry.

11. Paint the base unit now, before adding the countertop.

12. Glue the countertop to the bottom, making sure the spigot is at the back. Weight down to ensure a good bond. Let dry.

13. Turn the unit on its back and glue beads to front doors and drawers for pulls if desired.

Wooden Beads

Small painted or varnished wooden beads, available in hobby shops, can be used to make decorative stool and table legs and even posts for beds and étagères. Strung on tiny dowels or florist wire and glued together, they look like real hand-carved or lathe-turned pieces.

To ensure that your items are sturdy, choose beads that are smooth and regular and that fit snugly on the dowel or wire used. Little macrame beads work particularly well because they will fit on a relatively heavy dowel. If you are stringing beads on a dowel or wire that is smaller than the bead holes, wrap some paper around the dowel to ensure a snug fit. Also, be sure the beads are securely glued to one another as well as to the dowel.

FOOTSTOOL

This easy little piece of furniture makes a nice accent for a dollhouse. The stool can vary in height, depending on the style of sofas and chairs it is complementing. The one pictured in figure 38 is approximately one

FIG. 38: Wooden beads have been used here to create the stool and coffee-table legs, as well as the shelf dividers of the étagère.

inch square and one inch high, but you can alter these dimensions to suit your own needs.

The footstool is constructed simply by stringing small beads on wire to form legs and then gluing these to the bottom of a cardboard-reinforced pillow. The piece shown was fashioned from 1/2-inch-long and 3/16-inch-long varnished macrame beads and red velvet. Directions for making it follow.

MATERIALS NEEDED:

four beads 1/2 inch long and 1/4 inch in diameter
eight beads 3/16 inch long and 1/4 inch in diameter
four inches of florist wire or toothpicks to serve as dowels
fabric scrap
multipurpose craft cement
thread
shoebox-weight cardboard
nylon stockings or kapok for stuffing

TOOLS NEEDED:

wire cutter or tin snips
scissors
needle
ruler

PROCEDURE:

1. For dowels, cut wire or toothpicks into four 7/8-inch-long pieces. (Use tin snips for toothpicks or wire cutter for the florist wire.)
2. String three beads on each dowel, with one longer bead centered between two shorter ones as shown in figure 38. Be sure to put glue on each bead, so the legs will be sturdy.
3. Cut a fabric rectangle 1 1/2 inches wide and 2 1/2 inches long. Right sides together, fold the fabric in half to form a rectangle 1 1/2 inches by 1 1/4 inches. Stitch two sides closed, using 1/4-inch seams, and turn the cloth envelope right-side out.
4. Cut a cardboard rectangle 7/8 inch square and slide it into the fabric envelope.
5. Pad the top of the cardboard with stuffing; keep adding it until the footstool top is firm.
6. Stitch the open seam closed by hand. To attach the legs, turn the stuffed unit upside down. Apply glue to the four corners of the pillow bottom and allow to become tacky. Then attach the legs and hold or prop up until dry.

TABLE LEGS

A variety of legs for low and high tables can be made from beads. Simply select a combination of beads that gives the look and height you want, string on a dowel or heavy wire, and attach to the tabletop of your choice. Tops can be parts from plastic and cardboard boxes, or sheets of balsa wood cut to the desired size and stained or painted. See the preceding section on balsa wood for details.

ÉTAGÈRE

Making an étagère is like stacking up several tables. Directions follow for the handsome one shown in figures 23 and 38; but by selecting and arranging beads in a different fashion you can easily design a unit of your own.

The étagère shown was created from varnished wood beads and balsa-wood shelves finished with wax-based shoe polish.

MATERIALS NEEDED:

sixteen wooden beads, 1/2 inch high
twenty-eight wooden beads 1/4 inch high
a balsa-wood strip 2 inches wide, 1/8 inch thick, and 18 inches long
florist wire or toothpicks to fit the holes in the beads
multipurpose craft cement
desired finishing material for shelves

TOOLS NEEDED:

wire cutter or tin snips
X-acto or razor-blade knife and supply of blades
ruler
fine-grit sandpaper

PROCEDURE:

1. From the balsa strip, cut out four rectangles, each 1 3/4 inches wide and 4 inches long, for shelves.
2. With sandpaper, smooth the edges of the balsa strips. Also round the four corners of the shelves if desired.
3. Apply the desired finish to the shelves and let dry (see the preceding section on finishing if needed).
4. Cut florist wire or toothpicks into twelve 1-inch pieces for dowels. (Use tin snips for toothpicks and wire cutter for florist wire).

5. Using figure 38 as a guide, string and glue two smaller and one larger beads on each dowel. Carefully secure the beads to one another and to the dowel with glue. Let dry.

6. On the bottom of the lowest shelf, glue a larger bead to each of the four corners. Let dry.

7. To attach the second shelf, first glue four bead posts to the top corners of the first shelf. Then glue the second shelf on top of the bead posts. Make sure the second shelf is in line with the first. Prop up between bookends or blocks and let dry thoroughly.

8. Repeat this procedure for the third and fourth shelves. Let dry thoroughly.

9. Glue the four remaining small beads to the corners of the very top shelf.

CANOPY BED POSTERS

Beads can also be used to make the posters for a fancy canopy bed. Instructions for actually creating the rest of the bed are in chapter 3, "Furniture from Cloth and Stuffing."

Since the posters will be supporting the entire structure of the bed, be sure to select beads that fit together smoothly. You can make your posters exactly as shown in figure 21 and as described here, or beads of different sizes and shapes can be selected to achieve a different effect. But regardless of the beads used, remember that they *must* fit snugly on their dowels. If you find that the bead holes are too large, wrap the dowels with strips of paper to prevent the posters from wobbling.

MATERIALS NEEDED FOR THE POSTERS SHOWN:

thirty-two 1/4-inch-high wooden beads
twenty 1/2-inch-high wooden beads
heavy florist wire for dowels
multipurpose craft cement

TOOLS NEEDED:

wire cutter
ruler

PROCEDURE:

1. Cut four lengths of florist wire, each 5 1/4 inches long.

2. String eleven beads on each wire, using figure 39 as a guide. Be sure

71

FIG. 39: Canopy bedposts — directions for stringing beads.

that 1/2 inch of wire is left protruding at the ends. Glue beads carefully to one another and to the wire. Let dry.

3. After the base and canopy are attached by these bead posters, complete the posters by placing an additional 1/2-inch bead at the top and bottom of each wire.

FIG. 40: All the cabinet pieces in this traditional room are constructed from simple cardboard boxes, decorated with lace trim, and then given an antique finish.

5

Furniture from Cardboard Boxes

*C*ardboard boxes are readily available and are very useful in making dollhouse furnishings; in fact, these materials can be turned into a whole array of interesting furniture — from simple end tables and storage cubes to elegant "antique" desks, buffets, grandfather clocks, and other cabinet items (see figure 40).

In some projects, closed boxes — those with all six sides intact — are needed. For others, "lidless" containers are required.

Simple Cardboard Furniture

If you have a collection of small cardboard containers on hand, the chances are good there are some pieces of simple furniture and appliances among them.

Perfume, jewelry, and notepaper boxes with plain or decorative exterior finishes are an especially good source of "ready-made" furniture. Used as is, a plain box can be an end table, tabletop, headboard, or storage cube. By gluing in strips of balsa wood for shelves, you can turn a box into a bookcase. Or look for containers with interior compartments -- these provide instant shelf space. A set of cardboard boxes can even be glued together and used as a wall unit.

With just a bit more modification, cardboard containers can also readily serve as stoves, washers and dryers, and television sets. Directions for making these follow.

TELEVISION SET

The television cabinet in figure 41 is made from a small "lidless" box. The front of the set is constructed from cardboard covered with aluminum foil. A slide mount and snap fasteners are glued on the foil to suggest the screen and controls.

FIG. 41: A television set with bobby-pin antenna.

The television set shown in the photograph was made from a boxtop 2 3/4 inches long, 2 inches wide, and 3/4 inch deep. However, since televisions come in a variety of sizes, any small box with similar dimensions will do.

MATERIALS NEEDED:

one small "lidless" box or boxtop
one 35 mm color-slide mount (available in photography shops)
shoebox-weight cardboard
aluminum foil
one small picture cut from a magazine
two sets of clothing snaps, one large and one small
one bobby pin
white household glue
brown wax-based shoe polish (optional)

TOOLS NEEDED:

scissors

PROCEDURE:

1. If desired, rub outer surfaces of the cardboard box with several coats of brown shoe polish to produce a wood-colored finish.
2. To make the front of the television, cut out a cardboard rectangle the same size as the opening in the box. Cover the cardboard piece with aluminum foil, neatly wrapping the edges of the foil around to the back of the rectangle. Set aside.
3. Separate the hinged front and back of the slide mount and discard one mat. Glue the picture from a magazine to the back of the remaining mat so that it can be "viewed" on the television screen. Let dry.
4. Glue the mounted picture to the front of the foil-covered rectangle for television screen. Set aside to dry.
5. For the antennae, make a small hole in the top of the television cabinet. Bend the bobby pin into a V and poke through the hole. Glue in place.
6. Glue the foil-covered cardboard screen-side out across the opening of the cabinet.
7. Glue clothing snaps in place on aluminum foil for controls, using figure 41 as a guide.

S T O V E

This project is made from a closed cardboard box reinforced with masking tape and covered with heavy opaque self-adhesive paper. The stove shown in figure 42 has a white exterior, but you can select other colors, such as avocado green or harvest gold, to match your dollhouse decor.

FIG. 42: This stove is made from a cardboard box covered with self-adhesive paper. "Electric" burners are flat wire spirals.

The oven door and back control panel are made from cardboard rectangles covered with self-adhesive paper. The "electric" burners are coiled strips of wire. The controls and clock are suitable pictures cut from a catalog. And the oven-door handle is a toothpick wrapped in a strip of aluminum foil.

MATERIALS NEEDED:

76

one cardboard box, approximately 3 inches high, 3 inches wide, and 2
   inches deep
shoebox-weight cardboard
masking tape
approximately 1/4 yard of heavy self-adhesive paper
narrow plastic-coated wire (telephone wire is ideal because the gray and
   red colors can be used to simulate off and on burners)
aluminum foil
one toothpick with rounded ends
small color pictures of a clock and a suitable control panel from a
   catalog or magazine
white household glue

TOOLS NEEDED:

scissors
ruler
tin snips

PROCEDURE:
1. Using scissors, cut out the following pieces from cardboard:
one rectangle 2 1/4 inches wide and 2 inches high for oven door
one rectangle the exact width of the stove and 1 inch high for stove-
   back control panel
2. Cut out the following pieces from self-adhesive paper:
one rectangle the exact width of the stove and slightly deeper from front
   to back to cover the top of the unit.
one rectangle the height of the box and long enough to wrap all the
   way around it, covering the four sides
one rectangle 2 3/4 inches wide and 2 1/2 inches high to cover the front
   of the oven door
one rectangle 1 inch wider than the stove and 3 inches high to cover the
   stove control panel
3. If the box used is lightweight cardboard, neatly wrap with masking
tape for reinforcement.
4. Cover the top of stove with the first rectangle of self-adhesive
paper. Smooth the excess paper down the front and back of the stove.
5. To cover front and sides of stove, lap the longest strip of self-
adhesive paper all the way around the unit, being sure the upper edge
of the strip meets the paper covering the stove top at the sides of the
appliance and so that the ends meet in the middle of the stove back.
6. To finish the oven door, cover the 2 1/4-inch-by-2-inch cardboard
rectangle with the self-adhesive rectangle 2 3/4 inches by 2 1/2 inches.
Lap the paper under on all four sides.

7. To finish the control panel, wrap the narrow cardboard rectangle with the paper rectangle, as shown in figure 43. This will leave a tab of

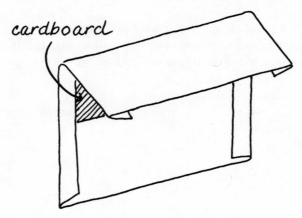

cardboard

FIG. 43: Stove — wrapping control panel.

paper at the lower edge of the control panel to help hold it to the stove.
8. Glue the control panel and oven door in place on the stove, using figure 42 as a guide. Tip the stove so the back of the control panel is on a flat work surface and weight down the stove front with a book or block. Let dry.
9. Make burners by coiling lengths of wire into flat spirals about 3/4 inch in diameter.
10. To make the door handle, cut about 1/4 inch from the ends of the toothpick. Wrap the remainder of the toothpick in a small strip of aluminum foil.
11. Glue burners, picture of controls, clock, and stove handle to the unit, using figure 42 as a guide.

WASHER AND DRYER

The basic construction of these two appliances is exactly like that of the kitchen stove just described, except that the finishing details are slightly different. Omit the burners, move the washer handle to the right side of the front door, and cut out suitable controls from catalogs or magazines.

"Antique" Furniture

You can make literally any cabinet piece your child's dollhouse needs by using a special "antique" construction process. Basically, the technique involves selecting a cardboard box to serve as a frame, wrapping it with masking tape, accenting the surfaces with heavy lace trim, and completely covering the cardboard and lace with an antique finish. Since projects are reinforced with masking tape and then finished attractively, they are as durable and appealing as the dollhouse furniture sold in toy shops.

By choosing the right box for the base and adding appropriate details, you can come up with an unlimited number of creative designs; for instance, one rectangular box can be a washstand, buffet, dresser, record cabinet, or desk. Two boxes stacked up will make a hutch, chest on chest, china cabinet, or storage unit. Insert matchboxes in the cardboard for drawers that really pull out and add hinges for doors that open.

Cabinet pieces without "moving parts" — those with simulated doors and drawers — are the easiest to make and are presented first in this section. It is a good idea to make several simple projects before trying the very detailed ones; but once the basic steps of the process are learned, the more complicated pieces are not really difficult — they just take more time and patience.

Selecting Containers

Lightweight cardboard boxes (toothpaste, rice, or dried-soup cartons, for example) make fine "frames" for cabinet pieces, but they must be reinforced with masking tape. In this step, strips of tape are simply wrapped neatly around the exterior surfaces of the container. To keep this from showing on the finished furniture, you can buy wide tape and trim it to fit. But narrow masking tape will not detract; rather, it produces an interesting boardlike texture on the surface of the final product.

Sturdy cardboard containers (notepaper or business-card boxes, for example) do not need reinforcement; however, if you're not sure whether the box selected is heavy enough, go ahead and wrap with tape. Otherwise your creation may warp when painted.

Remember that containers slightly larger than the size you need can usually be cut down and taped back together; or, for some projects, two smaller boxes of like size can be taped together and used as one. Also keep in mind that either closed or "lidless" boxes may be specified, depending on the project involved.

After the cardboard frame is prepared, lace trim is added to suggest a carved effect (see figure 44). This trim, which is sold in fabric shops either by the yard or in packages, comes in assorted widths, patterns, and colors.

FIG. 44: *The desk and the buffet shown here have been decorated with lace trim but have not yet been painted and antiqued.*

When choosing lace trim, carefully consider basic shape and design. You will need both wide and narrow trims to achieve the kinds of "woodworked" effects shown in this section. Wide designs are especially useful because they can be cut up to produce various narrow borders or single motifs (on desk drawers in photographs 44 and 45, for example).

FIG. 45: *This is how the pieces shown in figure 44 look after finishing.*

It isn't necessary to find lace patterns exactly like those used in the projects illustrated. Other designs of the same general type will create equally attractive results. And don't worry about the color of the trims, since none of the shades will show once the furniture is painted and antiqued.

Gluing

After selecting bits and strips of lace and arranging them on the box, attach permanently by using an ordinary white household glue, such as Elmer's. (Heavier details like bead legs and door knobs are glued on with a multipurpose craft cement like Bond 527.)

Finishing

When the glue is dry, the furniture piece is covered with two to four coats of either latex wall paint or acrylic craft paint. Latex wall paint covers with the fewest coats and has either a semigloss or flat finish. Acrylic craft paint has a matte finish. Regardless of the type of paint, lighter shades are preferable since they show off the antique effect best.

After the final coat of paint has dried, an antique finish is added. Use a metallic wax product such as Rub 'n Buff, a wax-based shoe polish, or a dark, scratch-covering furniture polish, such as Old English, and apply with a soft cloth or paper towel. Rub the surface lightly when using the metallic wax product or wax-based shoe polish. If you use furniture polish, apply generously and then carefully wipe off the excess. (When properly applied, the furniture polish will leave only a light film on the furniture surface.) In any case, be sure to work some of the antique finish into the pattern of the lace.

The scratch-covering furniture polish will produce a lightly toned antique look, and brown shoe polish, a medium finish. For a dark, heavy-antique effect, select a deep shade of metallic wax rub. These finishes can also be used in combination.

If you prefer, any of the commercial antiquing products (paint and dark top coat) can be applied to this furniture.

CHEST

The high chest shown in figure 46 can be used in a traditional bedroom. Since the drawers are simulated, it is very easy to create. All you have to do is glue lace trim to a closed cardboard box, add bead legs, and then cover with a paint and antique finish.

81

FIG. 46: *The high chest and nightstand are extremely easy to make from cardboard boxes.*

The chest pictured was covered with two coats of off-white semigloss latex wall paint and accented with a light application of dark, scratch-covering furniture polish (see preceding information on finishing for other types of looks).

MATERIALS NEEDED:

a closed cardboard box, approximately 4 inches long, 2 1/2 inches wide, and 1 3/4 inches deep
masking tape
heavy lace trim 1/4 to 1/2 inch wide
white household glue
multipurpose craft cement
light-colored latex or acrylic paint
desired antique finish
four opaque beads for chest legs

TOOLS NEEDED:

scissors
paint brush

PLATE 1: *An inviting dollhouse room featuring contemporary sofa and "antique" hutch.*

PLATE 2: *Dollhouse sitting room furnished in a comfortable Early American style.*

PLATE 3: *An elaborate armoire and velvet sofa can be the focal point in a formal setting.*

PLATE 4: *Charming bedroom with canopy bed and comfortable matching chair.*

PLATE 5: *A colorful, modern living room filled with sleek chrome and wood furniture.*

PLATE 6: *Inside the dollhouse. Eight full rooms of furniture you can make!*

PROCEDURE:

1. If the cardboard box is thinner than shoebox weight, reinforce by wrapping it with masking tape (see the introduction to this section for details). Carefully wrap strips of tape around all exterior surfaces of the box.
2. Decide which side will be the chest back and place it on a flat work surface. Using figure 46 as a guide, glue a decorative border of lace at the top and bottom of the chest sides and front with white glue. (The lace used need not be identical to that shown.)
3. To simulate drawers, use white glue to attach two additional strips of lace to the chest front only. Let dry.
4. Using multipurpose craft cement, glue beads to four corners of box bottom. Let dry.
5. Paint the entire chest, covering box, lace trim, and bead legs. Let dry and add at least one more coat of paint.
6. Apply desired antique finish (see introduction to this section for details on finishing, if necessary).

NIGHTSTAND

Follow directions for the chest just described, except use a closed cardboard box approximately 2 1/2 inches high, 1 3/4 inches wide, and 1 inch deep. Omit bead legs and decorate nightstand with lace trim as shown in figure 46.

HUTCH

The hutch pictured in figure 47 is produced from two cardboard boxes glued together. A "lidless" box, with balsa strips inserted for shelves, is stacked on top of a closed container, which serves as a base. Since its doors are only simulated with lace trim, the hutch is easy to make.

The hutch shown was finished with two coats of mint green semigloss latex wall paint and antiqued with bronze-toned metallic wax rub.

MATERIALS NEEDED:

a closed cardboard box, approximately 3 3/4 inches wide, 2 1/2 inches high, and 1 1/2 inches deep
a strip of balsa wood 1/2 inch wide, 1/8 inch thick, and at least 8 inches long

FIG. 47: "Antique" hutch created from two cardboard boxes.

a cardboard box top or "lidless" box, approximately 3 3/4 inches wide,
   3 inches high, and 1/2 inch deep
heavy lace trim 1/4 to 1/2 inch wide
white household glue
multipurpose craft cement
eight 1/2-inch beads for legs and top supports of hutch
four small beads or map pins for base-unit handles (optional)

paint and desired antique finish

TOOLS NEEDED:

scissors
ruler
X-acto or razor-blade knife
paint brush

PROCEDURE:

1. For hutch shelves, cut two pieces from the balsa-wood strip with an X-acto or razor-blade knife. Each piece should be 1/8 inch shorter than the width of the "lidless" box.
2. Using multipurpose craft cement, glue the balsa pieces into the "lid-less" box to create shelves. Let dry.
3. Using multipurpose craft cement, glue the hutch top and base unit together. Prop up and let dry.
4. With craft cement, glue four beads to the hutch top, spacing them evenly for decorative effect. (The beads will help support a top line of lace trim, as shown in figure 47.)
5. Using figure 47 as a guide, attach lace trim to the hutch with white household glue. Use the row of beads on the hutch top to support the uppermost line of lace. Let dry.
6. With multipurpose craft cement, glue four beads to the corners of the hutch bottom for legs. Let dry.
7. Paint the entire hutch, including all lace and beads. Apply at least two coats. Let dry and add desired "antique" finish.
8. With multipurpose craft cement, glue small beads or map pins to the hutch-base unit for door handles, if desired.

ORNATE BOOKCASE

Believe it or not, the charming piece shown in figure 48 was made from an ordinary rice box. But by adding a pediment, shelves, doors, "carved" ornamentation, and beads for legs, the basic structure is completely transformed.

As figure 48 shows, the doors of this bookcase are not hinged. Instead, they are made by cutting and bending flaps from the box itself. Of course, hinged doors can be substituted; or simplify the unit merely by simulating doors with lace trim.

The piece shown was covered with three coats of pale blue semigloss latex wall paint and finished with a heavy application of bronze-toned

FIG. 48: *This ornate bookcase with cabinet doors is made from an ordinary rice box.*

metallic wax rub. It stands about 8 inches tall, including the pediment and legs. Keep in mind that for a dollhouse with "low ceilings" the pediment and/or legs of the bookcase may have to be shortened slightly.

MATERIALS NEEDED:

a closed cardboard box, approximately 3 1/4 inches wide, 6 inches high,
   and 1 1/4 inches deep
shoebox-weight cardboard
masking tape
four 1/2-inch opaque beads for legs
heavy lace trim 1/4 to 1/2 inch wide
white household glue
multipurpose craft cement
paint and desired antique finish

TOOLS NEEDED:

scissors
X-acto or razor-blade knife
ruler
pencil
tracing paper
paint brush

PROCEDURE:

1. Lay the box on a flat work surface and draw two rectangles on the
front, using figure 49 as a guide. The upper rectangle (for shelves)

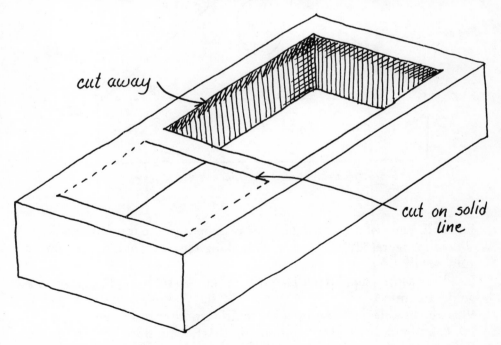

cut away

cut on solid line

FIG. 49: Ornate bookcase — cutting directions.

87

should be 2 3/4 inches wide and 3 1/4 inches high. The bottom rectangle (for doors) should be 2 3/4 inches wide and 1 1/2 inches high. Draw a vertical line down the middle of the lower rectangle to use as a cutting line for the cabinet doors.

2. With an X-acto or razor-blade knife, completely cut away the cardboard inside the upper rectangle to form the bookcase opening (see figure 49).

3. To form doors, cut through the horizontal lines of the lower rectangle. Then cut through the center vertical line on the lower rectangle. The doors will remain connected on each side (see figure 49).

4. To make bookcase shelves, cut three strips of cardboard, each 3 1/8 inches long and 1 1/8 inches wide. Wrap these shelves with masking tape for reinforcement.

5. With white glue and masking tape, fix the shelves in place. Let dry.

6. To reinforce the entire unit, carefully apply masking tape to all surfaces, including doors.

7. Using paper and pencil, trace the pattern for the bookcase pediment (figure 50). Transfer to cardboard and cut out. Bend cardboard at fold

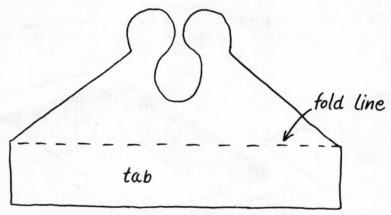

FIG. 50: Ornate bookcase — pediment-pattern piece.

line and, with white glue, attach the pediment to the top of the unit, as shown in figure 51. Add strips of masking tape to make the pediment fully secure.

8. With white glue, attach lace trim to bookcase, using figure 48 as a guide. Let dry.

9. Glue bead legs to unit by using multipurpose craft cement.

10. Paint bookcase and add antique finish. (For finishing details, see the introduction to "antique" furniture.)

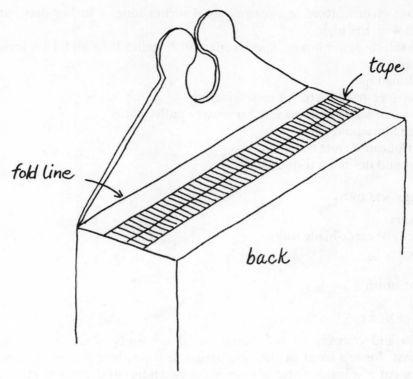

FIG. 51: *Ornate bookcase — adding pediment.*

ANTIQUE BUFFET

The buffet shown unfinished in figure 44 and finished in figure 45 has two drawers that actually open. These are made by inserting matchboxes into holes cut in the front.

For this project, use a sturdy "lidless" box. The opening will be at the back of the buffet, allowing you to manipulate the drawers during the construction process. If desired, you can close off the back of the buffet with a piece of cardboard or balsa wood once the unit is completed.

Although directions are given for a buffet, the same basic construction process can be used to produce a dresser, record cabinet, or washstand. You can even omit the matchbox drawers for an easier piece with the same general look. The buffet shown in figure 45 was finished with two coats of buff-colored, flat latex wall paint, covered with a light application of gold metallic wax rub.

MATERIALS NEEDED:

a boxtop or bottom, approximately 4 inches long, 2 inches deep, and
   2 1/4 inches high
two safety matchboxes, approximately 2 inches long and 1 3/8 inches
   wide
masking tape
heavy lace trim 1/4 to 1/2 inch wide
two small screw-and-nut sets for drawer pulls
white household glue
multipurpose craft cement
paint and desired antique finish

TOOLS NEEDED:

scissors
X-acto or razor-blade knife
pencil
ruler
paint brush

PROCEDURE:

1. To add drawers to the buffet, hold the ends of the matchboxes
against the top front of the box used and trace their outline in pencil.
Then cut just inside these lines to make two holes in the box front.

2. Push the matchboxes into these holes and secure in place inside the
buffet by using several thicknesses of masking tape.

3. Cut and apply lace trim to the exterior, as shown in figure 44, using
white glue. Let dry. Notice that the lace at the edges of the box front
was cut to make the pattern on the drawers and to outline the fake
doors at the bottom of the buffet; however, the lace used need not be
exactly the same as that pictured.

4. Glue bead legs to the corners of the buffet bottom with multipurpose
craft cement.

5. With scissors point, carefully make a hole in the center of each drawer
where the pull will be attached. (Be careful to keep each hole open when
painting and antiquing the buffet by repoking while the finish is wet.)

6. Remove the drawers, and paint and antique the buffet; be careful to
paint *only* the *fronts* of the drawers, or they will not slide in and out
when the buffet is dry. Wipe away any paint that drips into the drawer
openings. Let dry.

7. Add pulls by carefully pushing screws through the holes in the
drawers. On the inside, thread nuts on the screws and tighten. Put
drawers back in the buffet.

DESK

Made from ordinary matchboxes, the desk pictured unfinished in figure 44 and finished in figure 45 has nine drawers that actually open. Construction is fairly easy. First, the two side columns are put together. Then a center drawer is added, and a sheet of balsa wood is placed over the boxes to form a sturdy desktop. Lace trim and beads are glued on, and finally the unit is painted and given an antique finish. The desk shown in figure 44 was covered with two coats of flat buff-colored latex wall paint and finished with a heavy application of bronze metallic wax rub.

MATERIALS NEEDED:

nine matchboxes, approximately 2 inches long, 1 3/8 inches wide, and 1/2 inch high
a balsa-wood strip 4 1/4 inches long, 2 inches wide, and 1/8 inch thick
masking tape
heavy lace trim 1/4 to 1/2 inch wide
eight 1/2-inch beads for legs
nine small screw-and-nut sets for drawer pulls
white household glue
multipurpose craft cement
paint and desired antique finish

TOOLS NEEDED:

scissors
ruler
paint brush

PROCEDURE:

1. To reinforce the matchbox drawers, remove them and put strips of masking tape on the inside bottom of each drawer.
2. For each side of the desk, stack four matchboxes and carefully wrap them together with masking tape. Wrap the tape around them securely, but not so tightly that the "drawers" will no longer slide in and out.
3. With white glue, attach the center drawer between the two stacks, using figure 44 as a guide. Then wrap the sides and top of the nine-box unit with masking tape. Work carefully so that the drawers will still open and shut.
4. With multipurpose craft cement, glue the balsa-wood rectangle to

the top surface of the desk. Turn the desk upside down on a flat work surface and weight it down with a block or small book. Let dry.

5. With multipurpose craft cement, glue four beads to the bottom of each matchbox column. Let dry.

6. Using white household glue, attach lace trim to the desktop and edges, as shown in figure 44. Also cut bits of lace to fit the drawer fronts and glue in place, using the same photograph as a guide.

7. Remove desk drawers. With a scissors point, make a small hole in the center of each drawer where the pull will be attached.

8. Paint the desk. Carefully work around the drawer openings and wipe away any paint that drips on the interior surfaces. Also, apply paint only to drawer fronts and backs so they will slide in and out of the desk when the paint is dry. While paint is still wet, repoke the holes in the drawer fronts.

9. Add desired antique finish to desk and drawer fronts (see introduction to this section on "antique" furniture for finishing details).

10. When finish is dry, add drawer pulls by pushing screws through the holes. On the inside of the drawers, thread nuts on the screws and tighten.

11. Replace all drawers in the desk.

CABINET

In this project, hinged doors are added to a cabinet piece. As figure 52 shows, the hinges are not only used to open and close the unit but also provide decorative interest.

FIG. 52: Cabinet with hinged doors.

The cabinet is made from a small "lidless" cardboard box, with a front-panel inset constructed from balsa wood. Added for durability, the balsa wood is divided into two narrow, stationary panels and two front doors.

Although they need not be as large as those pictured, it is important to select hinges that are wide enough to actually support the doors. Look for ones with at least a 1/4-inch metal overlap, which can be glued to the narrow stationary panels, and a 1/2-inch overlap, which can be glued to the doors. Most hobby and craft shops stock suitable small-hinge sets with decoupage materials.

The cabinet shown in figure 52 was finished entirely with decoupage supplies. It was first covered with two coats of teal blue acrylic paint, rubbed very lightly with dark antique finish, and then sprayed with a coat of decoupage varnish.

MATERIALS NEEDED:

a "lidless" cardboard box or boxtop, approximately 3 3/4 inches long, 2 1/2 inches high, and 1 3/4 inches deep
masking tape
suitable small hinges
a balsa-wood strip 4 inches long, 2 1/2 inches wide, and 1/8 inch thick
heavy lace trim 1/4 to 1/2 inch wide
white household glue
multipurpose craft cement
paint and desired antique finish

TOOLS NEEDED:

X-acto or razor-blade knife
ruler
fine-grit sandpaper (optional)
paint brush

PROCEDURE:

1. If necessary, reinforce the box by wrapping with masking tape.
2. Measure the open side of the box and cut a piece from the balsa strip the same height and 1/16 inch narrower than the width of this opening.
3. On a flat work surface, cut this balsa piece into four sections; form two stationary panels and two doors as shown in figure 53. Be especially careful that the stationary panels are wide enough to accommodate the hinges you are using.
4. With multipurpose craft cement, glue the stationary panels to the

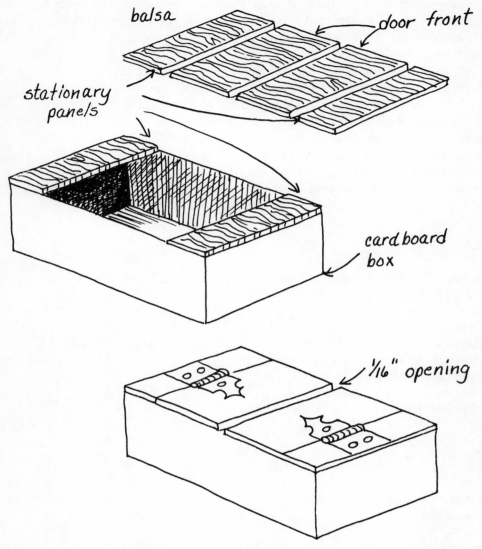

balsa

door front

stationary panels

cardboard box

1/16" opening

FIG. 53: *Hinged cabinet — cutting front panels, gluing on stationary panels, and gluing on hinges.*

vertical sides of the box opening, as shown in figure 53, and let dry.

5. Position the cabinet doors between the stationary panels. There should be a 1/16-inch gap in the middle so that the doors will still open easily after they have been painted. If they fit together too snugly, rub edges lightly with sandpaper or cut down very slightly and neatly with the X-acto blade.

6. Using figure 53 as a guide, position the hinges on the cabinet front

FIG. 54: *The handsome armoire shown has hinged doors and interior shelves*

and, with multipurpose craft cement, glue them to the stationary and door panels. Apply glue sparingly, being sure that it does not obstruct the movable parts of the hinges. Let dry.

7. Decorate the cabinet with lace trim as shown in figure 52. Note that in the unit pictured, a strip of lace covers the stationary panel and part of each hinge. Let cabinet dry.

8. Paint cabinet, being sure paint does not obstruct the movable parts of the hinges. Let dry and add at least one more coat.

9. Apply desired antique finish.

ARMOIRE

An elegant antique armoire with real hinged doors can be a focal point in almost any dollhouse. Construction of the piece shown in figure 54 and also in plate 3 is not really difficult but requires some attention to detail.

The frame of this armoire is a dried-soup-mix box. An opening is cut in the front of the box for the doors, which are each attached to the unit with two hinges. Balsa-wood strips are glued to the interior for shelves. Opaque beads serve as legs for the unit.

The piece shown was covered with two coats of beige semigloss latex wall paint and then rubbed lightly with bronze-toned metallic wax finish. The hinges, which were purchased in a craft shop, were covered along with the rest of the unit.

MATERIALS NEEDED:

a closed cardboard box, approximately 5 inches high, 4 3/4 inches wide, and 1 1/2 inches deep
a strip of balsa wood 24 inches long, 1 inch wide, and 1/8 inch thick for shelves
a strip of balsa wood 9 inches long, 2 inches wide, and 1/8 inch thick for doors
shoebox-weight cardboard
white household glue
multipurpose craft cement
masking tape
heavy lace trim 1/4 to 1/2 inch wide
two sets of suitable hinges (see directions on selecting hinges in cabinet project immediately preceding)
four 1/2-inch beads for legs
paint and desired antique finish

TOOLS NEEDED:

X-acto or razor-blade knife
scissors
fine-grit sandpaper
tracing paper
pencil
ruler
paint brush

PROCEDURE:

1. Lay the box flat on a work surface and, with a pencil and ruler, draw a 4-inch square on the center front. With scissors, carefully cut away the square of cardboard.
2. To reinforce the armoire, neatly wrap masking tape around all exterior surfaces of the box.
3. Cut the narrow balsa-wood piece into strips to form the armoire

shelves. Either use figure 55 as a guide, or make a simple set of shelves by cutting three or four strips to fit the interior.

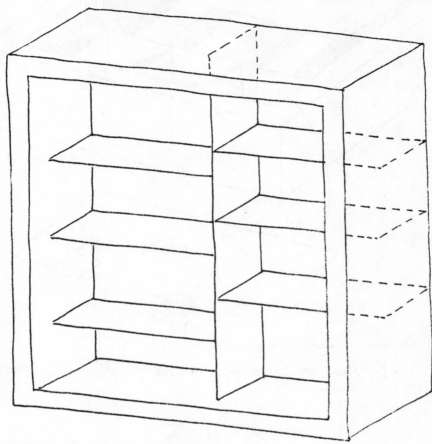

FIG. 55: Armoire — shelf construction.

4. Using multipurpose craft cement, glue the shelves into place. Let dry.
5. For doors, cut two 4-inch lengths from the wider balsa strip. Smooth the edges of the door pieces with sandpaper. Sand down until a 1/16-inch center gap is left when the doors are in place on the armoire (see figure 56).
6. Place two hinges 1 3/4 inches apart on the outer edge of each door front and glue down by using multipurpose craft cement. Let dry.
7. Position the doors in the opening of the armoire and glue the hinges to the armoire sides by using craft cement. Check to be sure the doors open and close freely. Let dry.

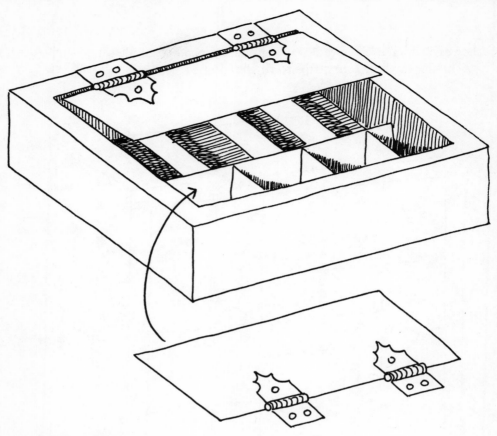

FIG. 56: Armoire — attaching hinges and doors.

8.   With paper and pencil, trace the pattern for the pediment (figure 57).

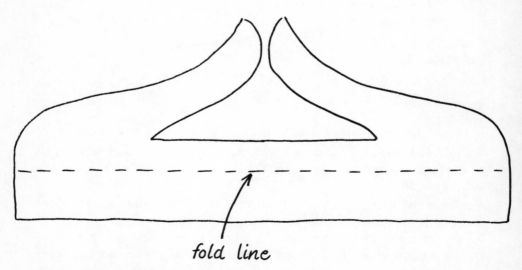

fold line

FIG. 57: Armoire pediment-pattern piece.

Transfer to cardboard and cut out. Bend cardboard at fold line and, with white household glue, attach pediment to top of armoire. Add strips of masking tape to make the pediment fully secure.

9. With white household glue, attach lace trim to the armoire as shown in figure 54 or as desired. Let dry.

10. Attach bead legs, using multipurpose craft cement. Let dry.

11. Paint the unit. Be sure the finish does not obstruct any movable parts of the hinges. Let dry and apply at least one more coat. Add desired antique finish.

GRANDFATHER CLOCK

A grandfather clock is not an essential item for a dollhouse, but it does make a charming and decorative addition.

The clock pictured in figure 58 is constructed from an ordinary toothpaste box. The face is a toy pocket watch. Other materials include two oblong wooden beads strung on an inexpensive jewelry chain for clock weights, a gold button hung from metallic-coated string for the pendulum, and a rectangle of transparent plastic from a greeting-card box for the "glass" window.

The clock shown was finished with two coats of off-white semigloss latex wall paint, accented with a heavy application of bronze-toned metallic wax rub.

MATERIALS NEEDED:

a discarded toothpaste box at least 5 1/4 inches high, 1 1/2 inches wide, and 1 1/2 inches deep
a toy pocket watch or suitable toy wristwatch
see-through plastic top from a greeting-card box
shoebox-weight cardboard
suitable inexpensive metal jewelry chain for weight pulls
suitable oblong beads for weights
metallic coated string
rounded gold button with a shank
heavy lace trim 1/4 to 1/2 inch wide
multipurpose craft cement
white household glue
masking tape
paint and desired antique finish

TOOLS NEEDED:

tracing paper

FIG. 58: Grandfather's clock made from a toothpaste box.

pencil
X-acto or razor-blade knife
scissors
ruler
paint brush

PROCEDURE:

1. Using scissors, cut away one end of the toothpaste box so that the remaining portion measures 5 1/4 inches high, 1 1/2 inches wide, and 1 1/2 inches deep.

2. On the cut-off end of the box, trim away a rectangle of cardboard 3/4 inch long and 1/4 inch high from the *center* of each side — this will form the clock legs, as figure 59 shows.

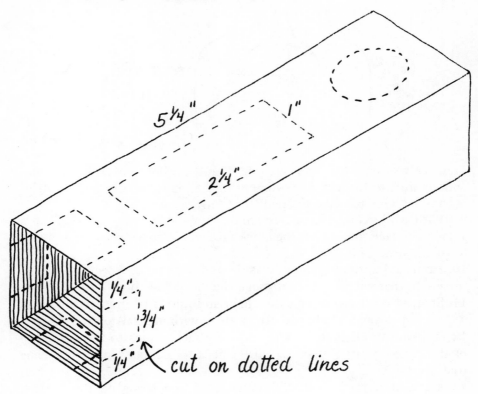

FIG. 59: *Grandfather's clock — cutting directions.*

3. To make the clock-front window, lay the box on its back on a flat work surface. With a pencil and ruler, draw a rectangle 1 inch wide and 2 1/4 inches high, starting about 1/2 inch from the box bottom (see figure 59).

4. To make the clock-face opening, center the toy watch on the top of the box. Trace around the watch on the cardboard.

5. Using the X-acto or razor-blade knife, cut away the clock-window rectangle on the lines drawn. Cut away the circle, just *inside* the line drawn.

6. Push the watch into the circle. If necessary, enlarge the hole size to

accommodate the watch. Using multipurpose craft cement, glue the watch into place. Let dry.

7. Carefully wrap all exterior cardboard surfaces with masking tape. Also, working from inside the box, add several strips of tape to help hold the watch in place.

8. With paper and pencil, trace the clock-pediment pattern (figure 60).

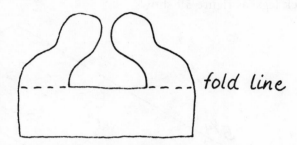

FIG. 60: Grandfather's clock — pediment-pattern piece.

Transfer to cardboard and cut out. Bend cardboard on fold line and, with white glue, attach the pediment to the top of the clock. Add strips of masking tape to make the pediment fully secure.

9. With white glue, attach lace trim to the clock, using figure 58 as a guide. The lace that circles the clock face will have to be cut and pieced to fit smoothly. Let dry.

10. Paint and antique the clock as desired. Be sure to finish the part of the inside that will be visible through the "glass" window.

11. String the "weights" on the chain and knot the ends. If the chain will not fit through the beads, attach them with neutral-colored thread.

12. Working through the open window, attach chains to the inside top of the clock by using masking tape. Check to see that the weights hang free from sides.

13. Tie a knot in the metallic-coated cord and string on the button. Slide the button down to the knot and glue into place to complete the pendulum.

14. Working through the open window, attach the pendulum to the inside top of the clock, using masking tape.

15. With scissors, cut a rectangle 1 1/2 inches wide and 3 1/4 inches high from the plastic greeting-card boxtop. Cut 1/4-inch-wide strips of masking tape. Place strips around the edges of the plastic, overlapping 1/8 inch on all sides.

16. Working from inside the bottom of the clock, position the plastic over the window opening. Press the masking tape against the interior sides of the clock, adjusting the tape to prevent it from showing in the window. Proceed carefully until window is in place.

102

6

Furniture from Plastic

P *lastic* is a versatile dollhouse furniture-construction material. With it you can create attractive pedestal tables, bucket chairs, headboards, and clothes trees. However, it is also possible to produce some more mundane household fixtures like tubs, sinks, toilets, and kitchen and bathroom cabinets by using plastic parts.

Assembly of plastic components is easy if the right kind of glue is used. Either a white household glue, such as Elmer's, or a quick-drying craft cement, such as Bond 527, worked well for all of the projects in this chapter. If the plastic you are using will not bond with either one of these adhesives, ask your local craft shop or hardware store to recommend an alternative product.

"MOLDED PLASTIC" TABLE AND CHAIR SET

The table and chairs shown in figure 61 are intended for the dollhouse playroom or child's bedroom. The set is made from an opaque plastic bottle and styrofoam spool. The neck of the bottle forms the table base. The bottom of the container is the tabletop. And the backs of the two chairs are cut from the bottle sides. Each chair seat is half of the styrofoam spool. The bottle used to make the set shown in figure 61 was a nine-ounce container of Earth Born cream rinse.

FIG. 61: "Molded plastic" table-and-chair set for the dollhouse playroom.

MATERIALS NEEDED FOR TABLE:

one opaque plastic bottle, about 2 1/4 inches in diameter at the bottom
   and 6 inches tall
multipurpose craft cement

TOOLS NEEDED:

ruler
scissors
medium-grit sandpaper

PROCEDURE:

1. For the tabletop, cut off the bottom of the bottle, working about
1/8 inch from the base. Since the cut edge will form the rim of the tabletop, try to cut as evenly as possible. Smooth any nicks with sandpaper
if necessary.
2. For the table base, cut off the top 1 1/8 inches of the bottle. Sand cut
edge if necessary.
3. Place the tabletop upside down on a flat work surface. Glue the cut
edge of table base to the top and let dry.

MATERIALS NEEDED FOR CHAIRS:

a styrofoam spool, about 1 1/4 inches high
opaque plastic (use the sides of the bottle from which the preceding
    table was constructed)
scrap of felt
multipurpose craft cement
transparent plastic tape
opaque plastic tape to match either the spool or plastic chair backs

TOOLS NEEDED:

ruler
medium-grit sandpaper
scissors
X-acto blade
tracing paper
pencil

PROCEDURE:

1. With an X-acto blade, cut styrofoam spool in half to form the two
chair bases.
2. Transfer the chair-back pattern piece in figure 62 to a piece of paper
and cut out. For each chair back, hold the pattern against the bottle
side and outline it by scratching the plastic with the point of the X-acto
knife. With scissors, cut out the chair backs.

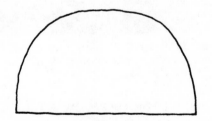

FIG. 62: Child's chair — pattern for back.

3. Attach chair backs to base by wrapping with a strip of transparent
tape. For a more finished look, cover this tape with an additional strip
of opaque plastic tape trimmed to fit the height of the chair base.
4. Cut out two felt circles 3/4 inch in diameter. Glue to spool tops for
chair cushions.

105

SMALL SHELF OR SPICE RACK

This shelf, shown in figure 63, is made from a large-size Gillette Trac II razor-blade dispenser. Simply remove the used blades and clean the dispenser. It can sit on a countertop or hang on the wall. Attach to the wall with folded pieces of masking tape under the opaque side of the back and folded strips of transparent tape under the clear side.

FIG. 63: On the wall of this dollhouse kitchen are a spice rack, made from a plastic razor-blade dispenser, and a hinged cabinet, made from a plastic pin box.

KITCHEN OR BATHROOM WALL CABINETS

These cabinets, shown in figure 64, are made from small-hinged plastic boxes in which pins and other sewing notions are sold. If shelves are desired, glue in strips of balsa wood cut to fit. Finish the exterior of your cabinet with two or three coats of spray paint or self-adhesive paper. To create a bathroom cabinet, glue on a small pocket mirror or a piece of aluminum foil cut to fit.

For permanence, attach the cabinets to the wall with multipurpose

FIG. 64: *Plastic pin boxes used for kitchen cabinets. The front of one box is covered with self-adhesive paper; the other is spray painted.*

craft cement. If heavy items will not be placed in the cabinets, they can be hung with folded strips of masking tape.

REFRIGERATOR

This basic piece of kitchen equipment is easy to produce from a hinged plastic box. Since refrigerators come in a variety of sizes, dimensions can vary. The refrigerator shown in figure 65 was made from a compartmented "fix-it kit," which originally held nails and tacks. A box without compartments could also be used by gluing in balsa-wood shelves. Directions follow for the refrigerator shown.

MATERIALS NEEDED:

a plastic box, approximately 3 inches wide, 5 inches high, and 1 1/2 inches deep
spray enamel paint (in white or a color to match your kitchen)
clip from a ball-point pen
multipurpose craft cement

FIG. 65: Refrigerator is a hinged plastic box coated with enamel paint.

TOOLS NEEDED:

tin snips

PROCEDURE:

1. Open the box and spray paint all *exterior* surfaces. Let dry and repeat. For best coverage, a third coat is recommended.
2. For the door handle, carefully pry off the clip from a ball-point pen. With tin snips, cut off the tiny prongs at the end and glue the clip to the refrigerator front with the rounded end pointing down.

BOOKCASE HEADBOARD

This modern bookcase headboard, shown in figure 66 is made from the bottom of a standard cassette-tape box, with a strip of balsa wood cut to fit the interior. First, separate the bottom of the box from the top. Then cut a strip of balsa wood 4 1/4 inches long and 1/2 inch wide. Finish the strip with black enamel or acrylic craft paint. Let dry.

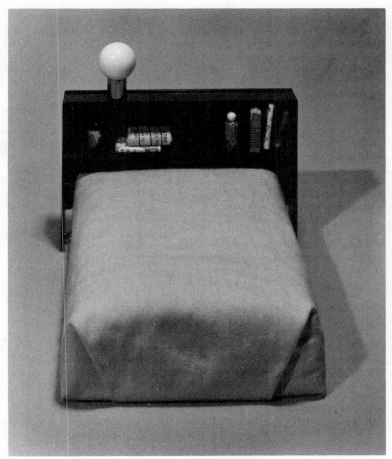

FIG. 66: *This simple-to-make modern bookcase headboard used to be the bottom of a cassette-tape holder.*

Position the shelf on the two interior supports and glue into place with multipurpose craft cement. The headboard will stand up by itself against a wall at the head of the basic bed described in chapter 3, "Furniture from Cloth and Stuffing."

CLOTHES TREE OR TOWEL RACK

This handy accent piece, shown in figure 67, is made from the small tree found in a 3 1/2-ounce jar of fancy olives. Using a pair of needle-nosed pliers, simply snip off all but the top four or five pairs of arms. Your rack is ready for dollhouse use.

FIG. 67: *Bathroom with towel rack, vanity, and toilet.*

TOILET

This essential piece of bathroom equipment can be put together quickly, using preshaped components. The bowl of the toilet shown in figure 67 is made from half of a child's plastic Easter egg. (This is similar to but much smaller than the plastic eggs in which stockings are sold.) The rounded end of a small, cylindrical, plastic bottle could be substituted. To make the base of the toilet, find a plastic bottle cap in which the bowl can sit. The tank of the fixture is a matchbox covered with heavy self-adhesive paper.

MATERIALS NEEDED:

half of a child's plastic Easter egg
suitable plastic bottle cap
matchbox, approximately 2 inches wide, 1 1/2 inches high, and 3/8 inch
    deep
opaque plastic tape (to match the egg being used)
heavy self-adhesive paper in a solid color

110

small piece of opaque plastic cut from a bleach or detergent bottle
white household glue
multipurpose craft cement
a seven-ounce plastic cup
hook from a large-sized hook-and-eye set

TOOLS NEEDED:

pencil
scissors
ruler

PROCEDURE:

1. To make the toilet seat, trace around the egg opening on the piece
of self-adhesive paper. Repeat the process to produce a second circle
exactly like the first. Cut circles out. Remove the backing from the
self-adhesive paper and place the circles, sticky sides together, to form
one unit. Place a quarter in the center of this circle and trace around it.
Cut away the resulting inner circle, forming the hole in the toilet seat.
2. To finish the toilet seat, cut the bottom from the seven-ounce plastic
cup, leaving 1/8 inch of the cup sides attached. Cut away a quarter-sized
circle from the center bottom of the cup. With multipurpose craft
cement, glue this rim to the bottom of the toilet seat, using figure 68
as a guide. This will hold the seat on the bowl. Set toilet seat aside.

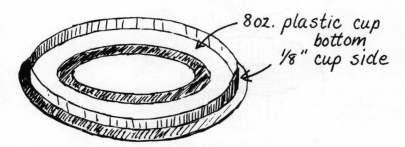

8oz. plastic cup
bottom
1/8" cup side

FIG. 68: Toilet seat and bottom rim.

3. Attach the egg half to the plastic cap with white household glue,
using figure 69 as a guide. If a good bond is not formed, reinforce with
a folded piece of plastic tape pushed inside the cap.
4. Cover the matchbox with self-adhesive paper, as if wrapping a
package. The seamless side of the wrapped box will be the tank front.
5. Cut a strip of plastic 1 1/2 inches long and 3/8 inch wide from the
bleach bottle. This will be used to fasten the matchbox tank to the bowl.

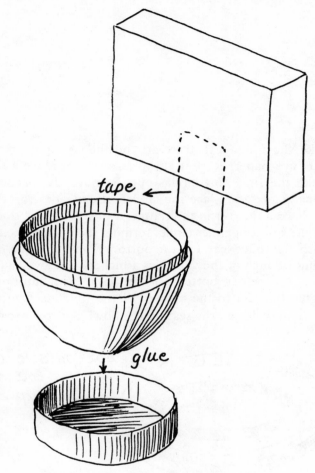

FIG. 69: *Toilet components.*

To attach, make a 3/8 inch slit with the scissors point in the underside of the matchbox. Slip the strip of plastic in the hole and glue into place. Let dry. (See figure 69.)

6. Attach the other end of the strip to the toilet-bowl back with a 1 1/2-inch piece of opaque plastic tape.

7. Attach the hook from the hook-and-eye set for the flushing handle with multipurpose craft cement, as shown in figure 67.

8. Set the toilet seat over the toilet bowl.

BATHROOM VANITY TOP

The sink-vanity top shown in figure 67 was made from a standard dimmer-switch plate found in a hardware store. Simply glue the plate to a suitable base. The sink bowl was produced from a plastic restaurant container in which individual jelly portions are served. The base shown was made from a plain cardboard box, with cabinet drawers drawn on by using a ball-point pen. However, a balsa-wood cabinet could be designed by following the general directions for balsa cabinetry in chapter 4.

Directions follow for the vanity top and cardboard base shown. A tiny seashell makes a nice soap dish.

MATERIALS NEEDED:

a dimmer-switch plate
a plain, "lidless," cardboard box, approximately 2 1/2 inches high, 4 3/8 inches wide, and 2 1/2 inches deep. (A taller box can be cut down to this height if necessary.)
a small, "lidless," plastic box for sink bowl. (The base of a seven-ounce plastic cup cut off 1/2 inch from the bottom could be substituted.)
a ball-point-pen clip for faucet
two small screw-and-nut sets for hot and cold taps
two small beads for holes in vanity top
two map pins (optional)
two small beads for cabinet doors
multipurpose craft cement
masking tape

TOOLS NEEDED:

scissors
ruler
ball-point pen
tin snips

PROCEDURE:

1. With a ball-point pen and ruler, draw cabinet doors on the front of the cardboard box. The top of the box should be the open side.
2. Turn the dimmer-switch plate upside down on a flat work surface and tape the sink bowl into position over the hole in the plate.
3. Turn the switch plate right-side up and glue it to the cabinet base. Let dry.

113

4. Glue small beads into the screw holes on the switch-plate top. Then, if you desire, glue map pins into the beads for stoppers. Let dry. These beads will appear to be cosmetic bottles.

5. To make the spigot, carefully pry the metal clip from a ball-point pen. Use a pair of tin snips to clip off the small prongs at the end. Then carefully bend down 1/8 inch at the rough end of the clip so it will hook under the edge of the vanity top. Attach the clip to the vanity top; glue into place and let dry.

6. Glue screw-and-nut sets to either side of the spigot for hot and cold taps. Let dry.

7. Turn the vanity-cabinet unit on its back. Glue bead door handles in place and let dry.

OLD-FASHIONED BATHTUB

This footed tub is extremely easy to make. Simply cut the bottom from a discarded plastic thirty-two-ounce bottle of dishwashing liquid. Glue on plastic beads for legs. An Ivory Liquid bottle was used for the tub shown in figure 70.

FIG. 70: Two bathtubs — one traditional, one modern.

MATERIALS NEEDED:

an empty thirty-two-ounce bottle from liquid dishwashing detergent
four opaque plastic beads, each approximately 1/2 inch high
multipurpose craft cement

TOOLS NEEDED:

scissors

medium-grit sandpaper
ruler

1. Remove the label from the bottle and wash out carefully.
2. With scissors point, scratch a line in the side of the bottle about 2 inches from the bottom. Cut off the bottom of the bottle, using this line as a guide and working as evenly as possible.
3. Sand edge smooth.
4. Turn tub over and glue beads to four corners. Let dry.

MODERN TUB

This modern tub, shown in figure 70, is fashioned from a plastic refrigerator-storage container. The bottom of the carton serves as the body of the tub, and the lid is cut to form the rim.

MATERIALS NEEDED:

a plastic refrigerator container, approximately 3 1/2 inches wide, 5 inches
    long, and at least 1 1/4 inches high
multipurpose craft cement

TOOLS NEEDED:

scissors
ruler
medium-grit sandpaper

PROCEDURE:

1. With a scissors point, scratch a line in the side of the container about 1 1/4 inches from the bottom. Cut off the bottom of the container, using this line as a guide and working as neatly as possible. (A container 1 1/4 inches high can, of course, be used as is.) Sand any rough edges smooth. Tub body is now finished. Set aside.
2. To produce the rim of the tub, first make a mark 1 inch from each corner of the lid. With a scissors point, scratch a diagonal line between each of these points. Cut away the flat surface of the container top, working about 1/8 inch inside the raised rim, using figure 71 as a guide.

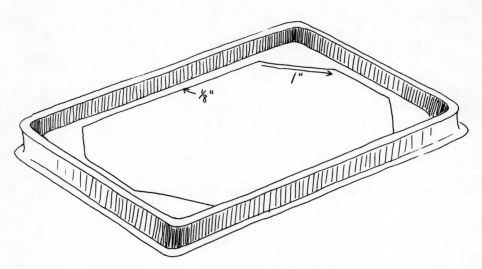

FIG. 71: Modern bathtub — cutting directions.

At the corners, follow the scratched lines, leaving   triangle in each corner. Sand any rough edges smooth. The cut-away portion of the top will look like an elongated octagon.

3. Glue the rim to the tub bottom and let dry.

7

Furniture from Metal

*D*on't overlook metal as a building material for dollhouse furniture. Tables, chairs, and sofas can be made from champagne cork wires, heavy galvanized wire, notebook-binder prongs, and large, square, paper clips called paper clamps. Simple construction techniques are used. In some cases, you can produce a chair or table frame just by bending these materials.

Many of the pieces in this chapter are sleek and modern in appearance; but the items made from champagne cork wires have an old-fashioned charm.

Champagne Cork Wires

The dull metal wires that hold champagne corks in their bottles can be used to make accent pieces with an 1890s look. It takes very little effort to turn these wire scraps into fancy boudoir stools, ice-cream parlor chairs, and tables.

Use tin snips to cut champagne cork wires where necessary. When gluing is called for, use a multipurpose craft cement, such as Bond 527.

FANCY BOUDOIR STOOL

Standing upright, champagne cork wires already look like a little stool. To complete the project, shown in figure 72, all you have to do is remove the horizontal wire around the "legs" and add a seat.

117

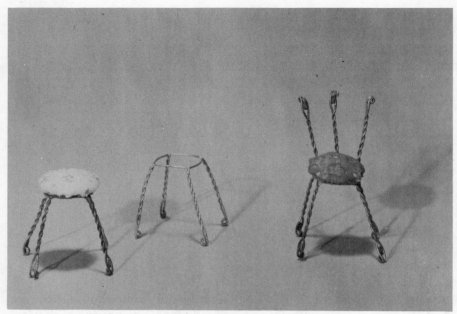

FIG. 72: *The stool and the chair are made from champagne-cork wires, like the ones shown between them.*

MATERIALS NEEDED:

wire from the cork of one champagne bottle
shoebox-weight cardboard
medium-weight fabric remnant
nylon stockings or kapok for stuffing
white household glue
multipurpose craft cement

TOOLS NEEDED:

tin snips
scissors
ruler
pencil

PROCEDURE:

1. With a pair of tin snips, cut and remove the horizontal wire that connects the "legs" of the stool frame.
2. For stool seat, make two circles of cardboard. For the first circle, trace around a quarter and, with scissors, cut away the cardboard just

118

outside the outline. For the second circle, trace around a nickel and, with scissors, cut away the cardboard just *outside* the outline.

3. Cut out a circle of fabric, about two inches in diameter.

4. Using white household glue, attach a small amount of stuffing to one side of the larger circle. Let dry.

5. Cover the stuffing with the fabric, carefully folding and gluing the raw edges to the underside of the cardboard.

6. To finish the underside of the seat, glue the smaller cardboard circle over the raw edges, tucking under and smoothing the fabric to obtain an even appearance. Press the small cardboard circle against the fabric with fingers until the glue becomes tacky. Let dry.

7. Using multipurpose craft cement, glue the seat in place on the frame. Let dry.

ICE CREAM PARLOR CHAIR

An authentic-looking ice-cream-parlor chair can easily be created with the wires from two champagne bottle corks. One set of wires serves as the legs and seat, and another is cut to make the chair back (see figure 72). For this project, use only *dull* metal wires from champagne bottles. Shiny aluminum wires are *not* suitable, since they cannot be bonded together satisfactorily. (Also see figure 73.)

FIG. 73: Dinette or patio set fashioned from champagne-cork wires.

MATERIALS NEEDED:

dull wires from two champagne-bottle corks
multipurpose craft cement
white household glue
shoebox-weight cardboard
medium-weight fabric remnant
nylon stockings or kapok for stuffing

TOOLS NEEDED:

tin snips
scissors
ruler
pencil

PROCEDURE:

1. With tin snips, cut and remove the horizontal wire that connects the four prongs on each set of wires. Turn one set with the prongs, or legs, down to form the chair base.

2. You will need three prongs from the remaining set to make the chair back. With tin snips, cut a wire section that contains two of the prongs and another section that contains only one prong. Be sure to include as much of the circular wire as possible so that the prongs can be glued securely to the chair base (see figure 74).

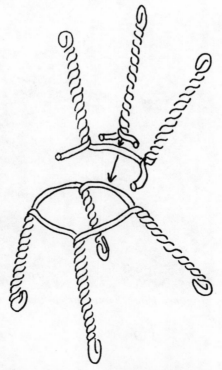

FIG. 74: Ice-cream-parlor chair — joining back to seat.

3. Glue the larger-pronged section to the chair base, forming the chair back. Let dry. Then glue the remaining prong to the middle of the chair back. Let dry.

4. To form the chair seat, make two circles of cardboard. For the first circle, trace around a quarter and, with scissors, cut away the cardboard just *inside* the outline. For the second circle, trace around a nickel and cut away the cardboard just *inside* the outline.

5. Cut out a circle of fabric, about 1 7/8 inches in diameter; it needn't be exactly round.

6. Using white household glue, attach some stuffing to one side of the larger circle. Be generous with the stuffing so that the chair seat will be plump when completed.

7. To finish the chair, follow steps 5 through 7 of the preceding project (*boudoir stool*).

ICE CREAM PARLOR TABLE

The base of the table shown in figure 73 is made by using the dull metal wires from two champagne-bottle corks. One set of wires is placed upright on its "legs," and the second is inverted and glued on top. Then a plastic or metal lid or round of cardboard is glued over the table base.

MATERIALS NEEDED:

dull wires from two champagne-bottle corks
suitable round 2 3/4 to 3 3/4 inches in diameter for tabletop
multipurpose craft cement

TOOLS:

tin snips
needle-nosed pliers (optional)

PROCEDURE:

1. With tin snips, cut and remove the horizontal wire that connects the four prongs on each of the sets of wires. Turn one set with the prongs down to form table legs. On a flat work surface, place the second set of wires with the prongs facing up. Using needle-nosed pliers or fingers, bend the four prongs out to right angles, approximately 1/4 inch from the ends. Adjust these ends if necessary so that the tabletop will be level when placed over them.

2. On a flat work surface, glue the top and bottom of the table base together. Let dry.

121

3. Check to make sure the tabletop sits horizontally on the table frame. Bend wires slightly if necessary. Glue tabletop to base and let dry.

Aluminum C-Prongs

Aluminum C-prongs, which are sold in stationery and office-supply stores for use in notebook binders, can be fashioned into modern table legs. These prongs are inexpensive, easy to bend, and easy to cut with tin snips. Legs for low tables can be made simply by cutting and bending 4 1/4-inch C-prongs to the desired shape; however, since long table legs need extra strength, these are made from pairs of metal strips glued flat sides together.

When gluing is required in the following projects, use a quick-drying epoxy, such as Devcon 5 Minute, or regular epoxy. To ensure strong bonding, metal surfaces being joined should be roughened with medium-grit sandpaper at the points of contact. Follow directions on the epoxy package and mix only a small amount at one time to avoid waste. Be sure to use glue sparingly. The appearance of your furniture will be neater, and the bond will actually be stronger. It is also important to let epoxy dry *thoroughly* before proceeding from one step to the next.

M - FRAME TABLES

Bases for modern end tables and coffee tables (see figure 75) can be made from C-prongs bent into the shape of Ms. For the tabletops, use cardboard jewelry box lids, balsa-wood strips, metal jar lids, or suitable coasters. Directions follow for the end table shown in figure 75. The top is made from a piece of balsa wood finished with one coat of brown wax-based shoe polish. For more information on balsa wood, see chapter 4.

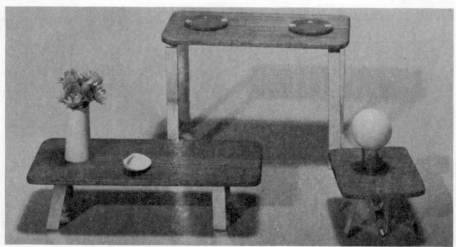

FIG. 75: *Modern coffee, dinette, and end tables with easy metal legs.*

MATERIALS NEEDED FOR END TABLE:

two C-prongs 4 1/4 inches long
quick-drying or regular epoxy
a strip of balsa wood 1 1/2 inches long, 2 inches wide, and 1/8 inch thick
brown wax-based shoe polish

TOOLS NEEDED:

ruler
tin snips
fine-grit sandpaper

PROCEDURE:

1. With tin snips, cut the pointed tips off two C-prongs. The metal strips will now each be 3 3/4 inches long.
2. To shape a strip into an **M**, first bend it in half to form a **V**. Then bend each side of the V down to form an **M**.
3. Repeat with the second strip to form the second **M**.
4. Prepare the tabletop by rounding the edges with sandpaper. Then finish by rubbing with brown wax-based shoe polish.
5. With the sandpaper, roughen the peaks of each M-leg unit where the tabletop will rest. Place the tabletop on the legs and check to make sure the surface is level. If necessary, adjust the legs gently by pulling out or pushing in the ends of the **M**s. Then glue the legs into place under the top as shown in figure 75 and let dry.

DINETTE OR SIDE TABLE

C-prongs, bent into the shape of **L**s, can also be used to make hall, dinette, dining-room, and side tables. Since the legs will be relatively long, they should be produced by first gluing pairs of C-prongs together. Tabletops can be made from cardboard, balsa wood, or metal jar lids. Directions follow for the side or dinette table shown in figure 75. The top is a piece of balsa wood, 2 inches wide and 3 1/4 inches long, finished with an application of brown shoe polish and then glued to the table legs. Additional information on working with balsa wood is provided in chapter 4.

MATERIALS NEEDED:

eight C-prongs, each 4 1/4 inches long
quick-drying or regular epoxy

a strip of balsa wood 4 inches long, 2 inches wide, and 1/8 inch thick
brown wax-based shoe polish

medium-and fine-grit sandpaper
tin snips
ruler

PROCEDURE:

1. Snip the ends off the C-prongs so that each strip is 3 inches long.
2. Roughen one side of each C-prong strip with medium-grit sandpaper. Sanded surfaces together, glue the strips in pairs to form four legs. For best results, use only a thin layer of epoxy between each pair of strips. Let dry thoroughly.
3. Bend each leg into the shape of an L; the longer part of each L should be 2 1/4 inches.
4. With fine-grit sandpaper, carefully round the corners of the tabletop. Then apply a coat of brown wax-based shoe polish.
5. Sand the surface of each L where it will be touching the underside of the tabletop. Use medium-grit sandpaper.
6. Lay the tabletop face down on a flat work surface and glue the legs into place so that the short lengths of the Ls face each other and are parallel to the ends of the table. Let dry.

"Chrome" Furniture from Wire

Heavy, fourteen-gauge, galvanized wire, available in hardware stores, is used for constructing the attractive modern sofa and chairs shown in figures 76 and 77. Because one continuous strip of wire is bent to make each separate frame, no gluing is necessary. Needle-nosed pliers with a wire-cutting attachment work well — both for cutting the wire and for holding the strip as it is bent into shape.

Since bending the wire to achieve the desired form *does* take precision, it is a good idea to practice with an unneeded strip before attempting any finished furniture. You will discover that the wire does not bend exactly where it is grasped. Instead, the bends will occur about 1/4 inch from the point of contact with the pliers.

After the supporting frames were completed, the sofa and chairs shown in figure 76 were finished with a cardboard-reinforced cushion unit.

FIG. 76: *This modern room features "upholstered" pieces with bent wire frames.*

FIG. 77: *A modern dining chair and the frame for a lounge chair of the same style.*

CHROME LOUNGE CHAIR

This chair is perfect for a modern dollhouse room. The frame is made from one continuous strip of galvanized wire. A reinforced cushion unit it then stitched into place. The chair shown in figure 76 was covered with a medium-weight cotton-polyester blend (see also plate 5).

MATERIALS NEEDED:

one package of fourteen-gauge galvanized wire
medium-weight fabric remnant
nylon stocking or kapok for stuffing
shoebox-weight cardboard
thread

TOOLS NEEDED:

needle-nosed pliers with wire cutter
scissors
ruler
needle

PROCEDURE:

1. Carefully unroll, straighten out, and (with wire cutters) snip off a strip of wire 11 1/2 inches long. (This may be slightly longer than you need; the excess can be cut off when the chair is finished.)
2. To construct the frame, use figure 78 as a guide. Start with point A and slowly make ten bends with pliers, ending at point J. The dimensions given in figure 78 must be duplicated as closely as possible. If necessary, the completed frame can be adjusted slightly with the fingers.

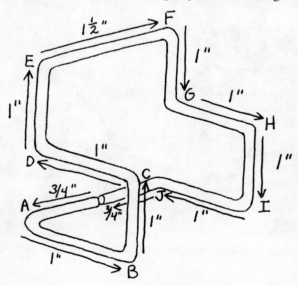

FIG. 78: *Chrome lounge chair — directions and dimensions for bending frame.*

3. For upholstery unit, cut out the following pieces with scissors:
one fabric rectangle 2 1/4 inches wide and 4 3/4 inches long
one cardboard rectangle 1 1/2 inches wide and 1 7/8 inches long
4. Fold the fabric piece, right sides together, to form a rectangle 2 1/4 inches wide and 2 3/8 inches long. Using a needle and thread, stitch the 2 3/8-inch-long sides 1/4 inch from each edge — this will form a fabric bag.
5. Turn the bag right-side out. Fold the cardboard reinforcement piece in half and insert it in the bag. Insert a small amount of stuffing into the bag on top of the cardboard to give the chair seat and back a soft, cushioned look. Then turn under the raw fabric edges and carefully stitch the bag closed by hand.
6. Arrange the seat unit on the chair frame. Whip stitch into place at top and bottom corners, as well as to the bottom back of the seat.

CHROME DINING CHAIR

This chair (see figure 77) is made exactly the same way as the lounge chair described above, except that the legs and back rest are slightly longer.

MATERIALS NEEDED:

one package of fourteen-gauge galvanized wire
scrap of medium-weight fabric
nylon stocking or kapok for stuffing
shoebox-weight cardboard
thread

TOOLS NEEDED:

needle-nosed pliers with wire cutter
scissors
ruler
needle

PROCEDURE:

1. Carefully unroll, straighten out, and (with wire cutters) snip off a strip of wire 12 1/4 inches long. (Any excess can be cut away when the chair is finished.)
2. To construct the frame, use figure 79 as a guide. Starting with point A, make ten bends with the pliers, ending at point J. Try to duplicate the dimensions given as closely as possible. If necessary, the completed frame can be adjusted slightly with the fingers.

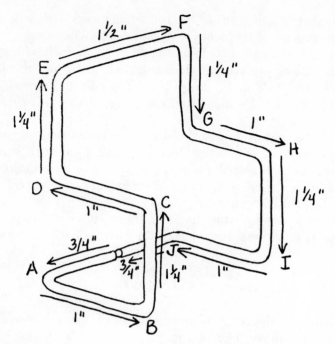

FIG. 79: Chrome dining chair — directions and dimensions for bending frame.

3. For upholstery unit, cut out the following pieces with scissors:
one fabric rectangle 5 1/4 inches long and 2 1/4 inches wide
one cardboard rectangle 1 1/2 inches wide and 2 1/8 inches long
4. Fold the fabric piece, right sides together, to form a rectangle 2 1/4 inches wide and 2 5/8 inches long. Using a needle and thread, stitch the 2 5/8-inch-long sides 1/4 inch from each edge — this will form a fabric bag.
5. To complete the chair upholstery, follow steps 5 and 6 under the previous project (*chrome lounge chair*).

CHROME SOFA

This sofa, shown in figure 76 and plate 5, is constructed in the same manner as the lounge and dining chairs just described.

MATERIALS NEEDED:

one package of fourteen-gauge galvanized wire
medium-weight fabric remnant
nylon stockings or kapok for stuffing

128

shoebox-weight cardboard
thread

TOOLS NEEDED:

needle-nosed pliers with wire cutter
scissors
ruler
needle

PROCEDURE:

1. Carefully unroll, straighten out, and (with wire cutter) snip off a strip of wire 18 inches long. (Any excess can be cut away when the sofa is completed.)
2. To construct the frame, use figure 80 as a guide. Starting with point

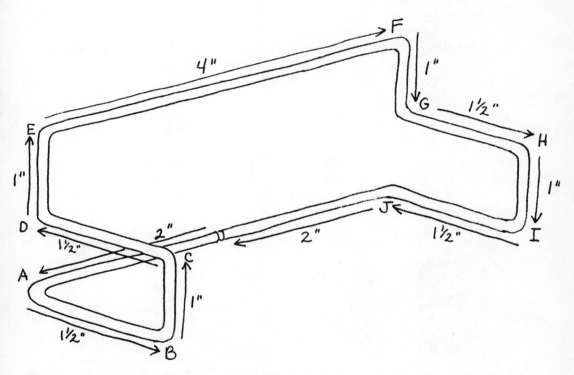

FIG. 80: Chrome sofa — directions and dimensions for bending frame.

A, make ten bends with the pliers, ending at point J. Try to duplicate the dimensions given as closely as possible.
3. For upholstery unit, cut out the following pieces:

129

one fabric rectangle 6 1/2 inches long and 4 3/4 inches wide
one cardboard rectangle 4 1/4 inches long and 2 3/4 inches wide
4. Fold the fabric piece, right sides together, to form a rectangle 4 3/4 inches wide and 3 1/4 inches long. Using a needle and thread, stitch the 3 1/4-inch-long sides 1/4 inch from each edge — this will form a fabric bag.
5. To complete the sofa, follow steps 5 and 6 under *chrome lounge chair.*

Paper Clamps

Large paper clamps (#2-size, squared-off paper clips), which are sold in stationery and office-supply stores, can also be used to make modern, tubular chair frames. The advantage of these clips is that the wire is already cut and is partially bent into the desired shape; however, since the metal is quite rigid, additional bends can be hard to make — even with needle-nosed pliers.

Two chair-frame designs follow. The second is produced from two paper clamps that are glued together with epoxy. If you enjoy working with these clamps, you can come up with more designs of your own, just by bending the metal into various shapes.

PEDESTAL DINING CHAIR

Like many modern dining-room chairs, this piece combines the clean, simple lines of metal with the soft, cushiony look of fabric (see figure 81). The pedestal-leg unit is formed from one paper clamp. The

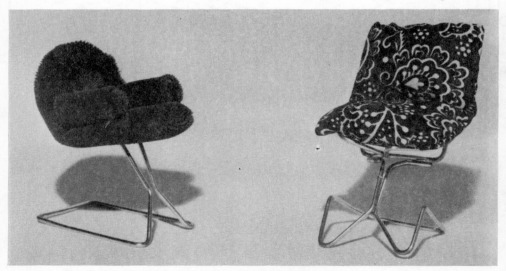

FIG. 81: Sleek pedestal dining chair and sling-back lounge chair.

upholstered part of the chair is made from a cardboard frame piece inserted in a fabric envelope and padded slightly. Chair arms are rolled fabric bolsters glued into place. Either a solid or printed medium-weight material can be used, although cloth with a sheen or nap will produce the most luxurious effect. The chair shown in figure 81 was covered with red velvet.

MATERIALS NEEDED:

one #2 paper clamp
thread
fabric remnant
shoebox-weight cardboard
discarded nylon stockings or kapok for stuffing
white household glue

TOOLS NEEDED:

needle-nosed pliers
needle
scissors
tracing paper
iron and ironing board
sewing machine (optional)

PROCEDURE:

1. With fingers, pull the two wings of the paper clamp open, as indicated in figure 82.

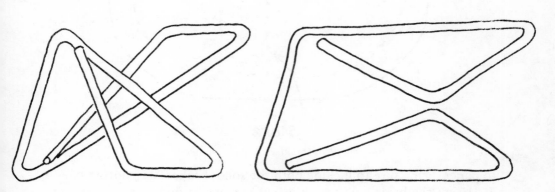

FIG. 82: Pedestal dining chair — directions for bending frame.

2. Pull up the two blunt ends to the position indicated in figure 83.

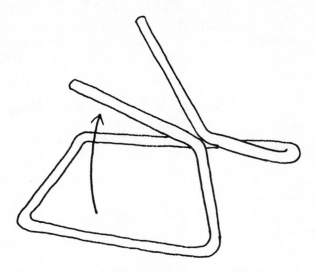

FIG. 83: Pedestal chair — additional bending directions.

3. With pliers, bend 3/8 inch of the blunt ends down to a horizontal position — this forms a base for the bottom of the chair seat.
4. For chair seat and upholstery, transfer the pattern given in figure 84

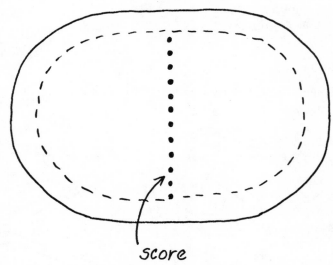

score

FIG. 84: Pedestal chair — pattern piece.

to paper, being sure to include both the solid, broken, and dotted lines.
5. Using the broken-pattern line, cut out one cardboard piece for seat-back frame.

6. Using the solid-pattern line, cut out two fabric pieces for seat-back frame upholstery.

7. Cut out two additional fabric rectangles, 2 inches long and 1 1/2 inches wide, for chair arms.

8. With a scissors point, score the cardboard seat-back frame piece as indicated by the dotted line on the pattern. Bend scored line gently to form a right angle.

9. Right sides together, stitch the fabric seat-back upholstery pieces together, using a 1/4-inch seam; leave one straight side of the upholstery open so the cardboard frame can be inserted.

10. Turn the upholstery envelope right-side out and slip in the cardboard piece. Bend the cardboard back to a "sitting" position. Insert a small amount of stuffing on top of the cardboard at the back and seat, smoothing to give a soft, even appearance. Stitch opening closed by hand.

11. For chair arms, lay the two fabric rectangles right-side down on a work surface. Fold in the raw edges of the longest sides 1/4 inch to form a strip 1 inch wide. Press raw edges down with an iron.

12. Roll up each strip to form a tube; only one raw edge of each tube will show. Using a needle and thread, take a few stitches along this raw edge to hold the bolster closed.

13. Place a line of glue along the raw edge and at one end of each tube. Using these glued edges, press the bolsters into place for chair arms, as shown in figure 81. Let dry.

14. Attach the chair base to the underside of the chair seat by sewing the wire ends to the fabric with a whipping stitch, as if attaching a large shank button. For additional stability, put a small amount of glue over the stitching. Let dry.

SLING BACK LOUNGE CHAIR

The frame of this chair, shown in figure 81, is made from two paper clamps and requires more bending than the dining chair in the previous project. One clamp forms the legs of the chair, while the other is used to make the seat and back. The two are then glued together with quick-drying or regular epoxy. Finally, a seat-back cushion unit is sewed to the frame by hand. The chair shown in figure 81 was covered with a medium-weight, cotton-polyester blend.

MATERIALS NEEDED:

two #2 paper clamps
quick-drying or regular epoxy

medium-weight fabric remnant
thread
discarded nylon stockings or kapok for stuffing

TOOLS NEEDED:

needle
medium-weight sandpaper
needle-nosed pliers

PROCEDURE:

1. To construct the seat-back of the chair frame, bend the ends of one paper clamp apart with fingers to the position shown in figure 82.
2. Then bend the two ends up to beyond a ninety-degree angle, as shown in figure 85.

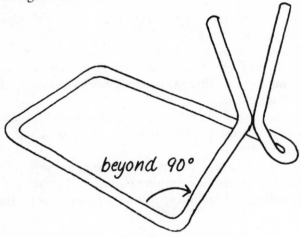

FIG. 85: Sling-back lounge chair — seat-back bending directions.

3. With pliers, bend the wire back to a ninety-degree angle, 1/2 inch from the ends, as shown in figure 86. The seat-back is now finished.

FIG. 86: Sling-back lounge chair — seat-back bending directions.

4. For leg unit, unfold the other paper clamp to the position shown in figure 82.

5. One inch from the squared-off end, bend the metal to a one hundred-degree angle, using pliers (see figure 87).

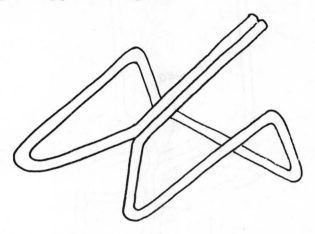

FIG. 87: Sling-back lounge chair — seat-base bending directions.

6. Bend the last 1/2 inch of the metal ends out and up slightly with pliers. If necessary, adjust the shape of these ends to conform to the bottom of the seat-back unit (see figure 88). Turn both paper clamps to position indicated in figure 89.

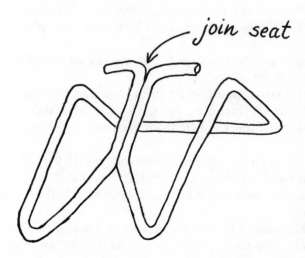

FIG. 88: Sling-back lounge chair — seat-base bending directions.

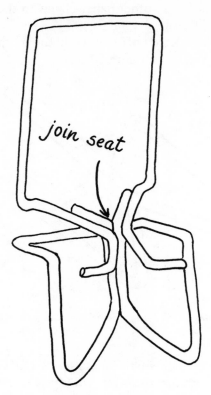

FIG. 89: Sling-back lounge chair — position of back and base for gluing together.

7.   Using sandpaper, roughen the seat area where the top and bottom clamps will be joined (indicated by the arrow in the illustration). Glue together with epoxy. Prop the chair until the glue is set. Let dry thoroughly.

8.   For seat-back cushion unit, cut a piece of fabric 6 1/2 inches long and 2 inches wide.

9.   Fold the fabric piece, right sides together, to form a rectangle 3 1/4 inches long and 2 inches wide. Using a needle and thread, stitch the 3 1/4-inch-long sides 1/4 inch from each edge — this will form a fabric bag.

10. Turn the pillow bag right-side out. Stuff very lightly. Turn raw edges under and stitch open side closed by hand. Then make a line of stitching across the middle of the cushion so it will bend to the contour of the chair.

11. Sew the cushion to the chair frame by hand with small whip stitches at the top and bottom corners, as well as the bottom back.

8

Accessories

A *ccessories* are the finishing touches for any dollhouse. Fill the little rooms with pictures, lighting fixtures, books, kitchen utensils, and planters. These details will help make the miniature world come alive. The more accessories you have, the more interesting and realistic the settings will be.

This chapter contains a number of simple projects to get you started. To include all the items that could be created would take another whole book. The possibilities are endless — and exciting. Once you begin making lamps, pictures, canisters, and magazines — like the ones described here — you'll probably be able to think up some designs of your own.

Don't overlook craft shops and catalogs as a source of ready-made accessories. Some of them sell inexpensive miniature animals, vases, flowers, and figures. Although these items are intended for special handicraft projects, they are fine for dollhouse use.

TRAYS

The metal pop-out lids from cocoa powder, dry mustard, and similar powdered products are ready-made trays for a dollhouse. Depending on the item purchased, the trays will be silver- or gold-colored, or enameled (see figure 90 for an example).

FIG. 90: An attractive display, including enameled tray and tiny bottles fashioned from beads.

FANCY BOTTLES

A collection of little bottles for dressing tables, sideboards, and other decorative uses can easily be made from pretty beads purchased in craft shops or taken from discarded necklaces. Select beads 1/4 inch or less in diameter.

The bottles can be fashioned from a single bead, with a map pin glued on for a stopper. Or glue several beads together for a more elaborate effect (see figure 90).

Jewelry studs or large sequins found in craft shops can serve as bases for these bottles.

Lighting

A surprising variety of lighting fixtures can be produced with very simple materials, such as shirt studs, beads, pen and pencil parts, and other small objects.

MODERN GLOBE TABLE LAMPS

Each of these sleek-looking lamps (see figure 91) is put together from

FIG. 91: Accessories shown are lighting fixtures — from very modern to traditional.

139

one round bead and the metal cylinder from the middle of a mechanical pencil or retractable ball-point pen. To make the lamp with the longer base, use the mechanical pencil cylinder; for the one with the shorter base, use the pen cylinder. Glue the bead to the lamp base with a multi-purpose craft cement.

TABLE LAMP WITH PLEATED SHADE

For the base of this lamp (shown in figure 91) use a token from a game set, such as Sorry or Parcheesi. For the shade, simply attach a toothpaste or other cap with white household glue.

HANGING GLOBE LAMPS

These simple lighting fixtures (see figure 91) can be created from beads. For each lamp, string a large, round bead on a piece of thin wire or thread. For an accent at the top of the lamp, use one or two small beads or a jewelry stud. Attach the lamp to the dollhouse ceiling with a thumbtack.

TIFFANY TYPE HANGING LAMP

The brass- or silver-colored cup at the bottom of a discarded lamp socket makes a perfect Tiffany-style lighting fixture for a dollhouse (see figure 2). String a small bead on a piece of thin wire or thread — these become the light bulb and the cord for the Tiffany shade. Attach the finished lamp to the dollhouse ceiling with a thumbtack.

BRASS CANDLESTICKS

These candlesticks (see figure 91) are shirt studs with the decorative jewels removed. To make the candles, simply twist a small piece of wax paper to form a tube and glue to the cup of the stud.

Kitchen Accessories

All of the items shown in figure 92 are extremely easy to make; in fact, some require no modification. The trash can is the top from a

FIG. 92: *Shown here are a toaster, soufflé dish, stirring spoon, brass canisters, and kitchen wastebasket.*

bottle of fabric softener. The brass canisters are inexpensive decorative bells sold in craft shops. The large kitchen spoon is a McDonald's Restaurant coffee stirrer with the end of the handle cut off. The soufflé dish is also a restaurant find — it's a plastic cream server with the top portion cut away.

The toaster is created from a replacement plug for an electrical cord. The plug prongs were clipped off with tin snips, and a piece of paper bread was inserted in the slot at the top of the appliance.

Wall Decorations

Just as in real houses, dollhouse walls look warmer and more inviting when they're filled with a collection of pictures and other decorations; but because the scale is small, dollhouse wall ornaments are easy and inexpensive to improvise.

LARGE WALL CLOCK

The clock shown in figure 4 is made from a small, gold-colored

141

cosmetic or earring box, with a clock face pasted on the front. The face was cut from a gift catalog. Although the clock shown is modern, a more traditional example could have been made by simply selecting a different picture. For still another look, cover a small box with wood grain or other suitable self-adhesive paper before adding the clock face.

LOCKET PICTURE

Old lockets make good dollhouse wall decorations. Just glue a small picture cut from a magazine into the ready-made "frame" (see figure 93).

FIG. 93: Use discarded jewelry as interesting dollhouse ornaments.

MODERN WALL PLAQUES

Discarded pieces of jewelry and charms are other sources of dollhouse wall ornaments. The Aztec plaque shown in figure 93 is a costume jewelry pin. The horse is a metal charm.

FABRIC PAINTINGS

Large dramatic "paintings," like the one shown in figure 2, can be fashioned from scraps of suitable fabric, glued over box lids.

Choose medium-weight woven material with either an abstract or realistic print. Spread a thin layer of white household glue over the top and sides of the box lid. Center and wrap a rectangle of fabric around the lid, pulling the raw edges to the back and gluing them down.

Reading Material

Dollhouse-size magazines and books (shown in figure 94) are easier to make than you might think. The miniature jacket covers are cut

FIG. 94: As this photograph shows, tiny books and magazines make a dollhouse look "lived in."

from magazine advertisements. Naturally, the replicas of books shown in ads for best-sellers can be used; but little pictures of cosmetic boxes, food products, and cigarette packs often look just as good. To simulate magazines, cut out rectangles about 3 inches wide and 1 1/2 inches high. Make sure a cover design will appear on the front when you fold the piece of paper in half lengthwise.

Books are made in the same way, except that the covers are glued around small rectangles of balsa wood. Use balsa 1/8 to 1/4 inch thick. Vary the height of your books as desired. Cut the balsa with an X-acto blade. Attach the jackets to the books with white household glue.

FIG. 95: The back of the dollhous

9

Building a Dollhouse

A handcrafted dollhouse is one of the nicest presents your children can receive. Not only does it provide endless hours of fun and entertainment for the young owners, but it is a family treasure that can be passed down for many generations.

However, building a dollhouse *does* take some basic carpentry skills, a few power tools, and a good deal of time. So if you think you'd like to make the one in this chapter, be sure to read through the directions and look at the illustrations before beginning.

The dollhouse pictured in figures 95 and 96 was designed by Lawrence

FIG. 96: Front of dollhouse, showing complete interior.

Tarbell with suggestions from Ruth Glick. The idea was to provide as much playing space as possible for the least amount of construction effort and expense.

Unlike most dollhouses, this one has been planned with the front wall, rather than the back wall, missing — this means that you will have to imagine the front door in front of the stairs where it is often located in real homes.

Except for the patio door in the kitchen, there are no side windows — to provide more wall space for furniture placement. Although the house is only two stories high in the back, the pitch of the roof provides space for an attic loft, where a playroom and den are located. Note that there is an opening cut in the attic floor to allow access to this upper story. The entry was requested by the Glick children who wanted a ready passageway to the upper story for their dolls.

In general, the interior of the dollhouse is, as much as possible, like a real home. Besides the two attic rooms, there are two bedrooms, a bathroom (with the front wall cut away), an upper hall, stairway, living room, dining room, and separate kitchen (see plate 6).

Throughout the house, the scale is 1 foot to 1 inch, except for the ceilings on the two lower floors. These are over nine inches high to make the rooms look more spacious and to permit easier rearrangement of dolls and furniture during play.

You may decide to undertake the project simply as a means of economy. The savings *will be* considerable, since fine commercial doll-houses can cost several hundred dollars. But keep in mind that the time spent crafting a sturdy, well-constructed product will also pay off in years of enjoyment.

Materials, tools, and procedure for making the basic house follow. Optional exterior trim and painting details are presented at the end of the chapter.

MATERIALS NEEDED FOR DOLLHOUSE:

a rectangle of A-D or better plywood, 15 inches wide, 37 inches long, and 1/2 inch thick, for first floor of dollhouse

a sheet of A-A or better birch plywood, 4 feet wide, 8 feet long, and 3/8 inch thick, for remaining walls and floors

a pine 1 by 3 (nominal — actually 3/4 inch thick by 2 5/8 inches wide), 6 feet long for stair risers

a round dowel, 3/16 inch in diameter and 3 feet long, for stair handrails and supports

plywood glue

a box of #2 finishing nails

a box of #3 finishing nails

TOOLS NEEDED FOR DOLLHOUSE CONSTRUCTION:

power saw — radial arm saw with plywood blade, or table saw with plywood blade. (A circular saw with plywood blade or a saber saw with metal cutting blade and cutting guide can be substituted if absolutely necessary.)

electric drill with 1/16-inch and 3/16-inch bits

electric sander with supply of fine- or extra-fine-grit sandpaper

hand plane

claw hammer

tape measure

pencil

PROCEDURE:

1. Cut and sand all dollhouse pieces listed.

From the 1/2-inch-thick plywood:

one first-floor 15 inches by 37 inches

From the 3/8-inch-thick birch plywood (see figure 97 for cutting layout):

one roof 19 inches by 40 inches

one right side wall 15 inches by 20 inches by 28 inches

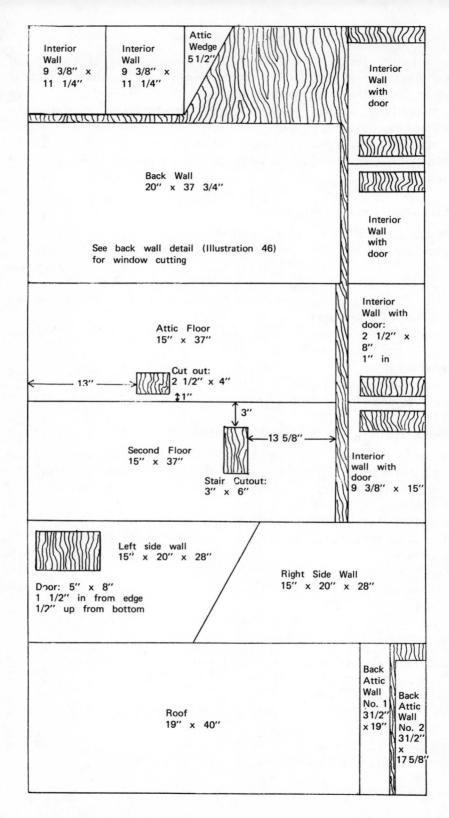

FIG. 97: Dollhouse cutting layout.

one left side wall 15 inches by 20 inches by 28 inches (with 5-inch-by-8-inch door cut out)

one back attic wall #1, 3 1/2 inches by 19 inches

one back attic wall #2, 3 1/2 inches by 17 5/8 inches

one second floor 15 inches by 37 inches (with 3-inch-by-6-inch stair opening cut out)

one attic floor 15 inches by 37 inches (with 2 1/2-inch-by-4-inch opening cut out)

four interior walls 9 3/8 inches by 15 inches (with 2 1/2-inch-by-8-inch door cut outs)

two interior walls 9 3/8 by 11 1/4 inches

one back wall 20 inches by 37 3/4 inches (with window cutouts, as detailed in figure 98)

one attic wedge wall 5 1/2 inches by 11 1/4 inches

From the pine 1 by 3:

fourteen stair risers, each 3 inches long

From the 3/16-inch round dowel:

seven vertical handrail supports, each 3 1/2 inches long

one handrail seven inches long

one handrail 3 inches long

Also drill 3/16-inch handrail-support holes in the second floor (see figure 99).

2. The dollhouse walls and floors are joined with #2 and #3 finishing nails driven through pilot holes and with plywood glue. When gluing, apply sparingly; a little goes a long way. Drill pilot holes for nails with a 1/16-inch bit about 3 inches apart, as shown in shaded areas of figures 98 through 102. The *X*s on the illustrations indicate possible pilot-hole locations. Drill holes as follows:

    In back wall, for all three floors and connecting walls, as shown in figure 98

    In floors, for all interior walls, as shown in illustrations 99, 100, and 101

    In side walls, for all three floors, as shown in figure 102

    In second floor, for left and center interior walls of first floor below.

    In attic floor, for 3 interior walls of second floor below.

3. To assemble the stairway (figure 103) the thirteen or fourteen steps will be sandwiched between the center, short interior wall and the right, longer interior wall. (The number of steps used will depend on their exact thickness; they are nominally 1 inch, but actually about 3/4 inch each.) When stacked, the steps must be *exactly* 9 3/8 inches high; if higher, plane the top step until the stack is the correct height. See figure 103 for step offset details. With #2 finishing nails and glue,

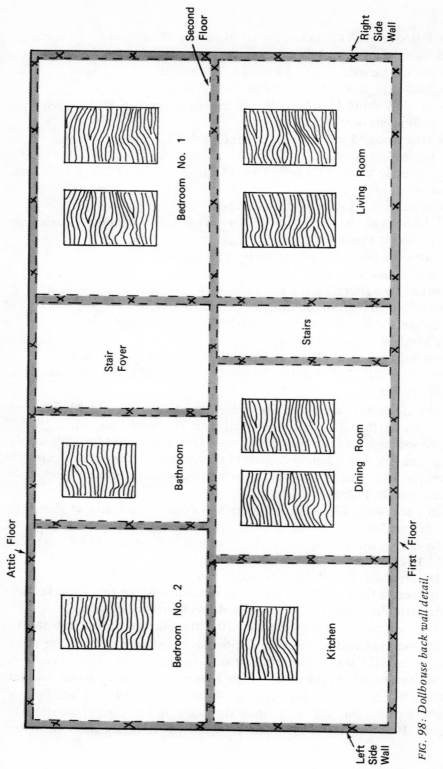

FIG. 98: *Dollhouse back wall detail.*

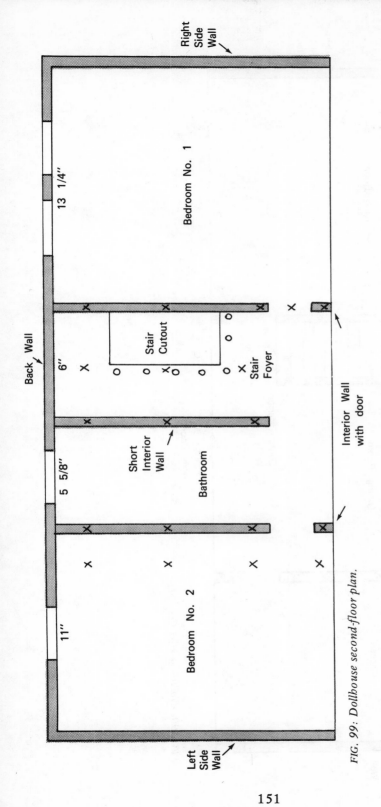

FIG. 99: Dollhouse second-floor plan.

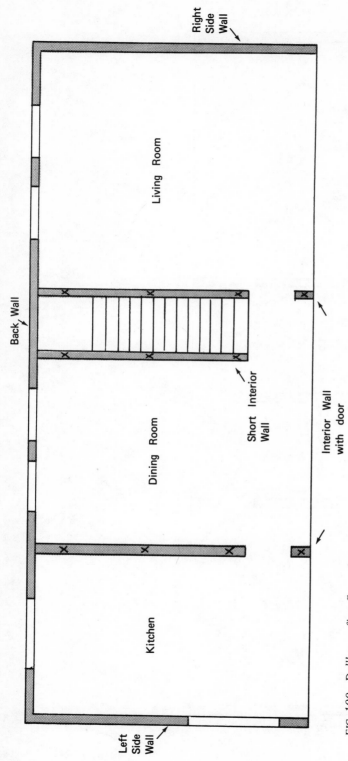

FIG. 100: Dollhouse first-floor plan.

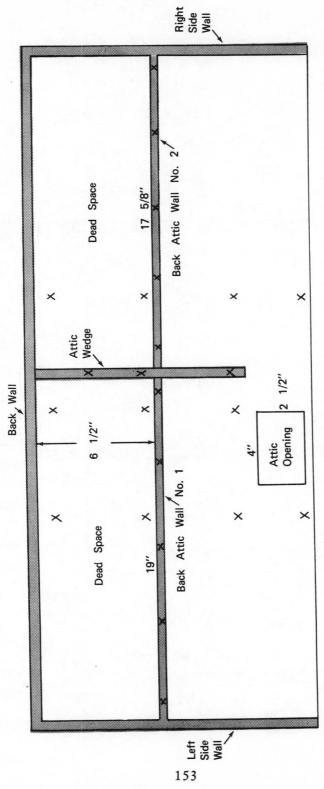

FIG. 101: Dollhouse attic floor plan.

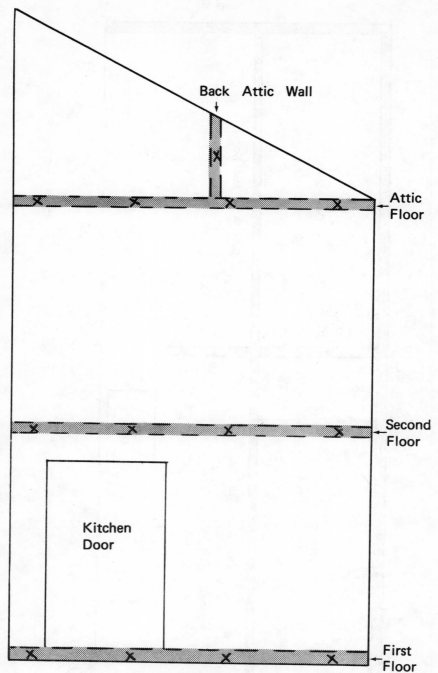

Back Attic Wall

Attic
Floor

Second
Floor

Kitchen
Door

First
Floor

FIG. 102: Dollhouse left side wall.

154

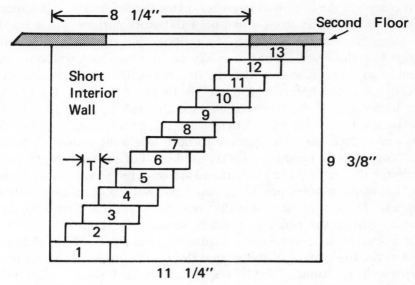

FIG. 103: Dollhouse stairway detail.

attach the steps to the center, short interior wall exactly as shown in figure 103. Start from the bottom and work toward the top. Before attaching the last step, measure the stack again to make sure it is the right height. Next, attach the right, longer interior wall to the other side of the stairway so that the back and bottom of both walls are exactly in line and square.

4. To complete the first-floor assembly (see figure 100), use #3 finishing nails and glue. On the top surface of the first floor, measure and, in pencil, mark all three interior-wall positions. Pilot holes already drilled should align with penciled markings for these walls.

Join the first floor and stairway-wall assembly as follows:

   Put a narrow line of glue on the bottom of both walls.

   Position assembly on first floor as marked. Attach assembly to floor by driving nails through pilot holes from beneath the floor.

Join the left interior wall to the first floor as follows:

   Put a narrow line of glue on the bottom of the wall. Position the wall on the first floor as marked. Attach the wall to the floor by driving nails through pilot holes from beneath the floor.

5. To complete side-wall assembly (figure 102), put a narrow line of glue on the *left* end of the first floor. Attach the left side wall to the first floor, as shown in figure 102, using #3 finishing nails driven through pilot holes in the bottom of the wall. Make sure that the floor and wall are exactly square. Then place a line of glue on the *right* end of the first floor and attach the right side wall in the same manner.

155

6. To complete the back-wall assembly, place the dollhouse, as it appears at this point, with its front down on a flat work surface. Put a line of glue along the back edge of the first floor, two side walls, and three interior first-floor walls. Then *carefully* position the back wall onto this assembly so that it is square with the first floor. *Be sure* the back wall is correctly oriented before placing it on the glued surfaces. Using pilot holes in bottom of the back wall, attach the wall squarely to the first floor with #3 finishing nails. Then, using pilot holes at each end of the back wall, attach the wall squarely to both side walls with #2 finishing nails. Note that #2 finishing nails are used in all of the steps that follow. Be careful that nails go in straight and are centered so side walls do not split. Using pilot holes provided, nail back wall to each interior first-floor wall. Make sure interior walls are exactly vertical. Stand the dollhouse upright; at this point it should be structurally stable.

7. To assemble the second-floor (figure 99), use #2 finishing nails and glue. On the top surface of the second floor, measure and mark all three interior-wall positions. Pilot holes already drilled should align with penciled markings for these walls.

Attach the 3 interior second floor walls to the second floor as follows:

Put a narrow line of glue on the bottom of each wall. One at a time, place the walls on the second floor as marked and attach to the floor by driving nails through pilot holes from beneath the floor.

Insert the second floor over the first floor as follows:

Put a narrow line of glue on the top of the first-floor interior walls, on the back of the second-floor interior walls, and on the back edge of the second floor. *Do not* put glue on the sides of the second floor. Carefully begin sliding the assembled second floor into place; insert it into the dollhouse a little too high and not quite touching the back wall. (This will prevent glue from smearing.) Then carefully slide the second floor down and back into place.

Nail the second floor to interior walls below as follows:

Using pilot holes already drilled, nail second floor to tops of interior walls below it. Note that only one nail can be put into the interior living-room wall because it is directly below the interior bedroom #1 wall; this one nail is put in the doorway of bedroom #1.

Nail the second floor to the side and back walls as follows:

Working from the outside through pilot holes already drilled, nail the second floor to side and back walls. Then nail the back wall to backs of three second-floor interior walls.

Insert handrail supports and handrail as follows:

Check to be sure the front edge of the top stair matches the back edge of the stair cutout in the second floor. (See cross-section in figure 103.) Glue the vertical handrail supports into holes already drilled. Then glue the two handrails into place. Allow handrails to dry completely before proceeding.

8. To assemble attic-floor (figure 101), use #2 finishing nails. On the top surface of the attic floor, measure and, in pencil, mark interior wall positions. Pilot holes already drilled should align with penciled markings.

Attach the attic wedge wall to the attic floor as follows:
Put a narrow line of glue on the bottom of the attic wedge wall. Position the wedge wall on the floor as marked. Attach to the floor by driving nails through pilot holes from beneath the floor.

Attach back attic wall #1 to attic floor as follows:
Put a narrow line of glue on the bottom and *right* side of the back attic wall #1. Position the wall against the attic floor and attach the wedge wall as marked. Attach back attic wall #1 to floor by driving nails through pilot holes from beneath the floor. Also drive one nail through the wedge wall into back attic wall #1.

Attach back attic wall #2 to attic floor as follows:
Put a narrow line of glue on the bottom and *left* side of back attic wall #2. Position the wall against the attic floor and attach the wedge wall as marked. Attach back attic wall #2 to the floor by driving nails through pilot holes from beneath the floor.

Insert the attic floor over the second floor as follows:
Put a narrow line of glue on the top of the second-floor interior walls and on the back of the attic floor. Carefully slide the assembled attic floor into place in the dollhouse, taking care not to smear the glue. The back of the attic floor should be flush with the top of the back wall.

Nail the attic floor to the second-floor assembly below as follows:
Using the pilot holes already drilled, nail the attic floor to the tops of the interior walls below. Then nail the attic floor to side and back walls, using the pilot holes already drilled. Attach each side wall to the corresponding back attic wall, using one nail driven through the pilot hole already drilled.

Prepare top edge of back wall for the addition of the roof as follows:
Plane the outside top edge of the back wall to match the slope of the two side walls and the attic wedge wall so the roof will fit properly.

9. To complete dollhouse assembly, the roof will be placed flush with the open, front side of the dollhouse and will overhang the back wall. It will overhang both side walls equally.

Drill initial roof pilot holes as follows:
Using a 1/16-inch bit, drill one pilot hole 1 inch from the front edge of the roof and 1 5/16 inches from the *left* edge of the roof. Drill another pilot hole 1 inch from the front edge of the roof and 1 5/16 inches from the *right* edge.

Determine additional pilot hole placements as follows:

Temporarily attach the roof to the dollhouse by using #2 finishing nails driven through the two pilot holes just drilled. Make sure the roof is properly aligned. Then, with a pencil, trace the position of the back wall, side walls, and interior attic walls on the underside of the roof. Remove roof.

Drill side wall, back wall and interior attic wall pilot holes as follows:

Using the pencil tracing as a guide, drill pilot holes about 3 inches apart for side walls, back wall, and interior attic walls with a 1/16-inch drill bit.

To permanently attach the roof to the dollhouse:

Put a line of glue on the top of the two side walls, the back wall, attic wedge wall, and two back attic walls. Carefully reattach the roof with #2 finishing nails driven through the two initial roof pilot holes; be sure the roof is correctly positioned and flush with the front edge of the side walls. Then, using the additional pilot holes just drilled, nail the roof to the dollhouse.

Of course, the exterior of the basic dollhouse described above can be finished in a number of ways. The easiest would simply be to apply a coat of neutral paint; however, with just a little more effort, you can achieve an extremely attractive effect.

As shown in figure 95, the dollhouse has been given a shingled roof, shutters, window trim, and "glass" windows.

The shingles are fashioned from rectangles of light cardboard, scalloped at the edges. After several coats of shellac and paint, they become very sturdy.

The shutters and trim are cut from strips of balsa wood, although flat molding can be substituted if you wish. The window panes are heavy transparent plastic.

MATERIALS NEEDED FOR DOLLHOUSE TRIM:

six manila folders for shingles
a pint of terra-cotta-colored latex semigloss wall paint for roof
a quart of buff-colored latex semigloss wall paint for walls
a can of spray shellac base coat for shingle sealer
a can of blue spray enamel for shutters
five sheets of *heavy* transparent plastic from notebook display sleeves
    for window "glass."
two strips of balsa wood 3 feet long, 1/2 inch wide, and 1/8 inch thick
    for window trim
two strips of balsa wood 3 feet long, 2 inches wide, and 1/8 inch thick
    for shutters

a plastic berry or cherry-tomato carton with decorative patterned sides
   for "lead glass" in living-room windows
white household glue
multipurpose craft cement

TOOLS NEEDED:

scissors
ruler
paintbrush(es)
X-acto or razor-blade knife and supply of blades

PROCEDURE:

1.   To make shingles, use scissors to cut manila folders into approximately 175 rectangles 2 inches wide and about 4 inches long. Scallop one edge of each rectangle so it will resemble three or four shingles.
2.   Starting at the bottom right edge of the roof, glue the shingle sets down in horizontal rows, using white household glue. Overlap slightly as you work. Also, slightly lap each successive row over the preceding one. Let glue dry.
3.   Give shingled roof several coats of spray shellac base coat. Let dry.
4.   Finish the roof with two coats of terra-cotta-colored paint. Paint only the top and edge of the roof surface. The underside of the overhang should be painted the same color as the exterior walls of the house. Let dry.
5.   Finish the exterior walls of the house and the underside of the roof overhang with two or three coats of buff-colored paint. Let dry.
6.   Before adding trim, tip over the dollhouse so that the windows will be facing up. Then cut a rectangle of transparent plastic 1/4 inch larger on all sides than each window. With multipurpose craft cement, glue each plastic rectangle over the appropriate window and let dry.
7.   Measure all windows and, with X-acto blade, cut trim from balsa wood strips to fit, using figure 95 as a guide. Narrow trim is cut from the 1/2-inch-wide strips. Shutters are cut down from the 2-inch-wide strips. The shutters on the double windows are 1 1/4 inches wide. The shutters on the other windows are 1 inch wide. (See chapter 4 for information on cutting balsa wood, if necessary.) Note that shutters are long enough to cover edges of narrow trim at window tops and bottoms.
8.   Spray shutters with two coats of blue paint. Cover narrow trim with one or two coats of terra-cotta paint. Let dry.
9.   While trim is drying, cut berry box apart at corners with scissors to

form four flat panels. Two panels positioned horizontally will be used to create the "lead glass" effect over one window pane (see figure 95). Cover panels with buff paint if desired and let dry. Then glue a pair of panels over windows with multipurpose craft cement, using figure 95 as a guide. Use glue at edges of panels only. Let dry.

10. Glue all trim and shutters to window edges, using figure 95 as a guide. Weight down if necessary and let dry.

11. When all trim is completely dry, stand dollhouse upright again.

For interior-finishing suggestions, see chapter 2, "Coordinating and Decorating."

Index to Projects

HOW THE HUMAN BODY WORKS

The Respiratory System

By Simon Rose

MEDIA ENHANCED BOOKS
AV2 BY WEIGL™
ADDED VALUE · AUDIO VISUAL

www.av2books.com

MEDIA ENHANCED BOOKS
AV²
BY WEIGL™
ADDED VALUE • AUDIO VISUAL

AV² provides enriched content that supplements and complements this book. Weigl's AV² books strive to create inspired learning and engage young minds in a total learning experience.

Your AV² Media Enhanced books come alive with...

Audio
Listen to sections of the book read aloud.

Key Words
Study vocabulary, and complete a matching word activity.

Video
Watch informative video clips.

Quizzes
Test your knowledge.

Embedded Weblinks
Gain additional information for research.

Slide Show
View images and captions, and prepare a presentation.

Try This!
Complete activities and hands-on experiments.

... and much, much more!

Go to www.av2books.com, and enter this book's unique code.

BOOK CODE

C 1 5 9 0 2 7

AV² by Weigl brings you media enhanced books that support active learning.

Published by AV² by Weigl
350 5th Avenue, 59th Floor
New York, NY 10118
Websites: www.av2books.com   www.weigl.com

Library of Congress Cataloging in Publication Data Available on Request

ISBN 978-1-4896-1178-9 (hardcover)
ISBN 978-1-4896-1179-6 (softcover)
ISBN 978-1-4896-1180-2 (single-user eBook)
ISBN 978-1-4896-1181-9 (multi-user eBook)

Printed in the United States of America in North Mankato, Minnesota
1 2 3 4 5 6 7 8 9 0 18 17 16 15 14

062014
WEP090514

Project Coordinator Aaron Carr
Art Director Terry Paulhus

Photo Credits
Every reasonable effort has been made to trace ownership and to obtain permission to reprint copyright material. The publishers would be pleased to have any errors or omissions brought to their attention so that they may be corrected in subsequent printings.

Weigl acknowledges Getty Images as its primary image supplier for this title.

Contents

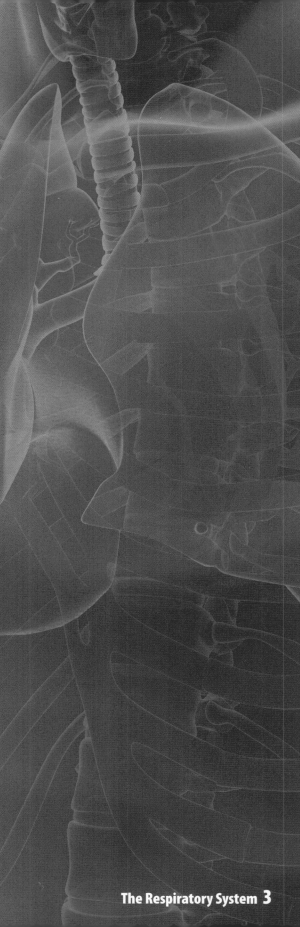

Human Body Systems

The human body is made up of many complex systems. Each one plays an important role in the way the body functions. These systems are also interconnected and work together.

For the body to stay healthy, all of its systems need to work together properly. Problems or diseases that affect one of the body's systems can also affect one or more other systems. More serious disorders tend to affect a greater number of systems.

6 MAJOR BODY SYSTEMS

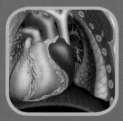

CARDIOVASCULAR SYSTEM

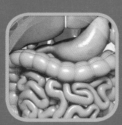

DIGESTIVE SYSTEM

MUSCULAR SYSTEM

NERVOUS SYSTEM

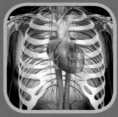

RESPIRATORY SYSTEM

SKELETAL SYSTEM

RESPIRATORY SYSTEM

Includes the lungs, airways, and respiratory muscles

Helps people to breathe air in and out

Supplies the body with the oxygen it needs

Rids the body of carbon dioxide

Connects with the cardiovascular system through the lungs

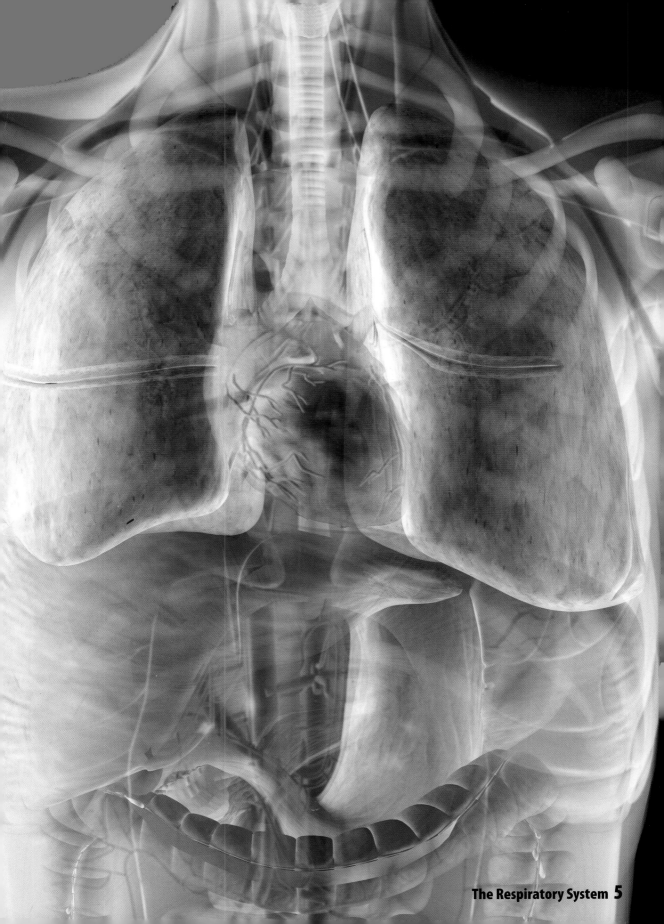

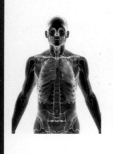

What Is the Respiratory System?

The lungs are the most important **organs** of the respiratory system. The system also includes airways, or passages, leading to the lungs. The muscles of the respiratory system include the **diaphragm** and the **intercostal muscles**.

The respiratory system provides the body with the oxygen it needs to survive. Oxygen makes up about one-fifth of air. Through the process of breathing in, the lungs take in oxygen. Through the process of breathing out, the respiratory system removes from the body waste products such as carbon dioxide gas.

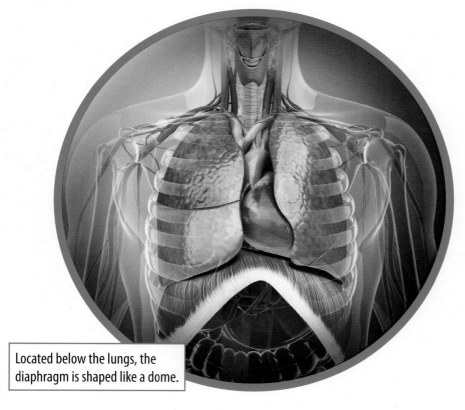

Located below the lungs, the diaphragm is shaped like a dome.

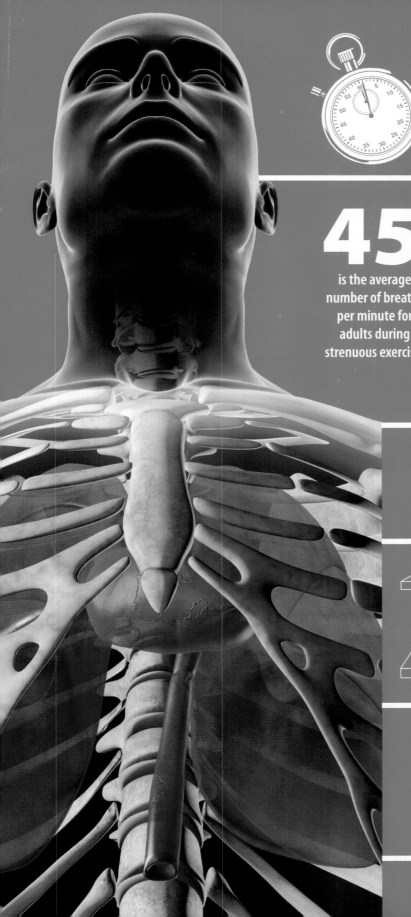

12 TO 20

is the average number of breaths per minute for adults not doing physical activity.

45

is the average number of breaths per minute for adults during strenuous exercise.

750 SQUARE FEET

(70 square meters) is the average surface area inside adult lungs.

There are **2** lungs in the body.

The lungs weigh, on average, slightly more than 2 pounds (1 kilogram).

400 CUBIC FEET

(11,000 liters) is the volume of air a person breathes in daily.

Respiratory System Features

The airways of the respiratory system bring air to the lungs and remove air from the lungs.

NOSE AND MOUTH Both the nose and the mouth take in air from outside the body.

PHARYNX Also known as the throat, the pharynx extends from the bottom of the nasal cavity and back of the mouth to the top of the larynx and **esophagus**.

LARYNX Also called the voice box, the larynx connects the pharynx to the trachea.

TRACHEA The trachea, or windpipe, transports air between the larynx and bronchi.

BRONCHI AND BRONCHIOLES The two bronchi branch from the trachea to enter each lung. The bronchi separate into many smaller tubes called bronchioles.

ALVEOLI Air sacs called alveoli, which look like bunches of grapes, are located at the ends of the smallest bronchioles.

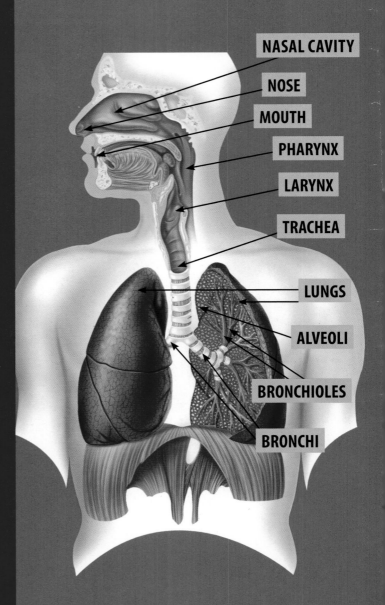

NASAL CAVITY

NOSE

MOUTH

PHARYNX

LARYNX

TRACHEA

LUNGS

ALVEOLI

BRONCHIOLES

BRONCHI

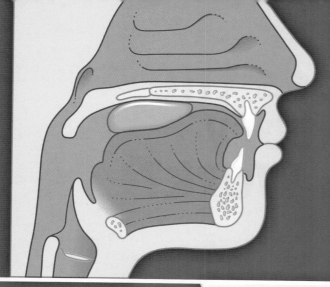

Nose and Nasal Cavity

The nose and nasal cavity make up the main outside opening of the body's respiratory system. Even when the mouth is closed, air is constantly entering and leaving the body through the nose. The nasal cavity is a hollow space behind the nostrils of the nose.

Mouth

Also known as the oral cavity, the mouth is the second outside opening of the respiratory system. Breathing through the mouth, as well as the nose, allows more air to enter the body. This is why people often breathe through the mouth while exercising, when the body's need for oxygen is greater.

Trachea

The trachea is about 4–4.7 inches (10–12 centimeters) long. It is a flexible tube. This allows the upper body to move while people are breathing.

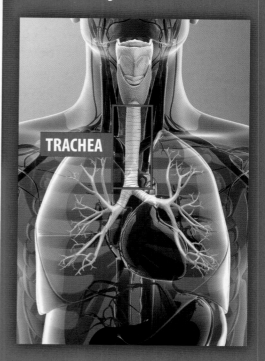

TRACHEA

Lungs

The lungs are among the largest organs in the human body. Located in the upper chest, they are protected by the ribcage. The action of the lungs allows people to talk and sing, as well as receive oxygen and get rid of carbon dioxide.

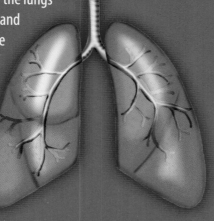

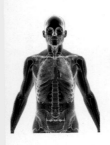

How Does the Respiratory System Work?

Respiration is the term for the process by which oxygen from the air is exchanged for carbon dioxide from the body. Breathing in is called inhalation, and breathing out is called exhalation. The diaphragm **contracts** to allow the lungs to expand when a person inhales. When the person exhales, the diaphragm expands to help force air from the body.

Air that is inhaled reaches the alveoli in the lungs. The human lungs contain millions of these tiny sacs. The walls of the alveoli have **blood vessels**. Oxygen from inhaled air is transferred to the blood flowing through these vessels. The blood then carries oxygen to the rest of the body.

As part of their normal functions, **cells** throughout the body produce carbon dioxide. This gas would be harmful to the body if not removed. As blood circulates, or travels, through the body, carbon dioxide from cells is transferred to the blood. When blood reaches the alveoli, the carbon dioxide is transferred from the blood to these sacs. It can then leave the body when the person exhales.

The Role of the Respiratory System

INHALATION Brings oxygen-rich air into the lungs.

EXHALATION Removes carbon dioxide from the blood and sends it out of the body.

REGULATION Adjusts the breathing rate as needed during times of greater or lesser activity.

Diagram of Gas Exchange

The process by which oxygen moves the lungs to the blood and carbon dioxide moves from the blood to the lungs is called gas exchange. This exchange occurs between the alveoli and the tiny blood vessels in their walls called capillaries. The capillaries and the alveoli walls share a membrane, which is a structure that allows certain substances to pass through it. Oxygen and carbon dioxide are carried in the blood by red blood cells. When these cells enter the capillaries of the alveoli, the carbon dioxide they were carrying moves through the membrane into the air sacs. Oxygen from the alveoli moves through the membrane and attaches to the red blood cells.

MEMBRANE

AIR WITH OXYGEN

AIR WITH CARBON DIOXIDE

from

ALVEOLI

CAPILLARY

BLOOD VESSEL CARRYING OXYGEN

BLOOD VESSEL CARRYING CARBON DIOXIDE

BRONCHIOLE

Bronchioles and Alveoli

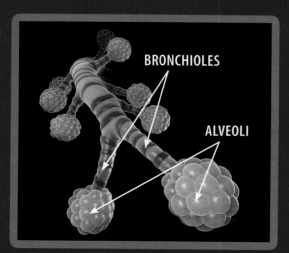

BRONCHIOLES

ALVEOLI

600 million
There are 600 million alveoli in a person's lungs.

1,000 miles
If all the capillaries in a person's lungs were placed end to end, they would be 1,000 miles (1,600 km) long.

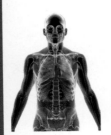

The Nose and Nasal Cavity

Inhaled air is cleaned as it passes through the nose and nasal cavity. In addition, cold air is warmed in the nasal cavity, before it enters the other airways and the lungs. The nasal cavity also adds moisturize to inhaled air, which helps keep the lower airways from becoming too dry. There are many blood vessels inside the walls of the nasal cavity. Heat and moisture are transferred from the blood flowing through these vessels to the inhaled air.

To clean inhaled air, the nasal cavity is lined with a thin layer of **tissue** called a mucous membrane and with tiny hair-like structures called cilia. **Mucus** and the cilia trap dust, **pollen**, and other materials before they can travel to the lungs. The cilia help to push harmful substances either toward the nostrils, where they are blown or sneezed out, or to the pharynx. From the pharynx, these substances enter the digestive system to be sent out of the body.

The upper part of the nasal cavity controls people's sense of smell. Special structures pick up odor-carrying particles from the air. Then, nerves send messages to a part of the brain called the olfactory bulb.

Using signals from nerves in the nasal cavity, the brain recognizes the smell of flowers.

The NOSE AND NASAL CAVITY by the Numbers

10,000
The nose can recognize about 10,000 different smells.

100
A sneeze travels at 100 miles (160 kilometers) per hour.

10 MILLION
The number of nerve cells in the nasal cavity.

Diagram of the Nose and Nasal Cavity

The nose is composed of bone, **cartilage**, muscle, and skin. A wall of cartilage separates the two nostrils. The palate, which is made of bone, separates the nose from the mouth.

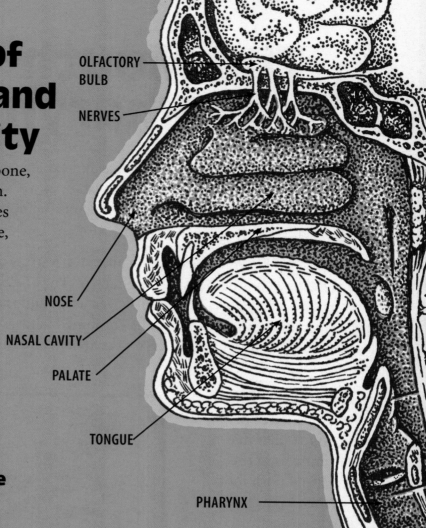

OLFACTORY BULB

NERVES

NOSE

NASAL CAVITY

PALATE

TONGUE

PHARYNX

Mucous Membrane in the Nose

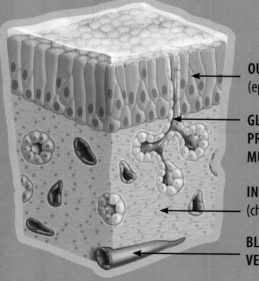

OUTER LAYER (epithelium)

GLAND THAT PRODUCES MUCUS

INNER LAYER (chorion)

BLOOD VESSEL

Air Sinuses

The air sinuses are hollow areas in the skull that open into the nasal cavity. Mucus produced in the sinuses drains into the nasal cavity.

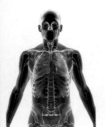

The Mouth and Pharynx

The mouth can help the nose to inhale and exhale. However, the mouth does not warm inhaled air or add moisture as well as the nose does. In addition, the mouth has no cilia or mucous membranes that clean the air before it goes to the lungs.

The nasal and oral cavities meet at the pharynx. Masses of tissue called tonsils are located on the sides of the pharynx. They help the body fight infections. The pharynx carries food as well as air and is part of both the respiratory and digestive systems. The combined pathway divides at the bottom of the pharynx. The larynx carries air, and the esophagus transports food.

Muscles of the Pharynx

There are two kinds of muscles in the pharynx. Circular muscles in the wall of the pharynx push food down to the esophagus and also help keep air from being swallowed. Muscles that extend lengthwise lift the pharynx up while a person is swallowing.

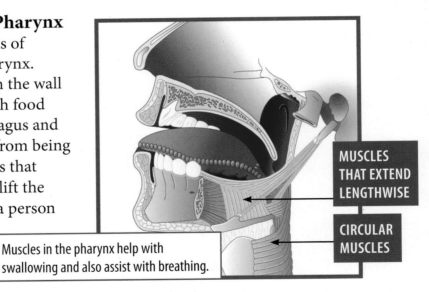

MUSCLES THAT EXTEND LENGTHWISE

CIRCULAR MUSCLES

Muscles in the pharynx help with swallowing and also assist with breathing.

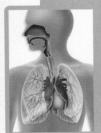

The MOUTH AND PHARYNX by the Numbers

5
The pharynx is 5 inches (13 cm) long.

10 MILLION
A person takes about 10 million breaths in a year.

2
A person has two tonsils.

Diagram of the Mouth and Pharynx

A small flap of tissue called the epiglottis covers the larynx when a person swallows. This prevents food and liquid from traveling to the lungs. The epiglottis is made mostly of cartilage.

MOUTH

TONGUE

PHARYNX

EPIGLOTTIS

LARYNX

ESOPHAGUS

Tonsils

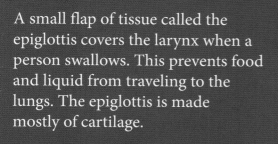

TONSILS

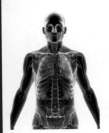

The Larynx and Trachea

The larynx is a box-shaped organ made mostly of muscle and cartilage. Besides assisting with breathing, it plays a major role in speaking, singing, and other sounds people make. The larynx contains a pair of mucous membranes called the vocal cords. They can vibrate when a person exhales, producing sound. The space between the vocal cords is called the glottis.

The length and thickness of the vocal cords can vary. These differences affect the way people's voices sound. Women and children tend to have shorter and thinner vocal cords than men. As a result, women and children often have higher-pitched voices, while men tend to have deeper voices.

The Trachea's Role

The trachea is located partly in the neck and partly in the chest. Stiff cartilage in the trachea's wall keeps this airway open at all times to allow air to pass through. Like the nasal cavity, the inside wall of the trachea is lined with a mucous membrane and cilia to stop dust and other harmful substances from traveling to the lungs. The trachea divides at the bottom into two tubes, one leading to each lung.

Singers learn to control the flow of air through their vocal cords to help produce the sounds listeners enjoy.

The LARYNX AND TRACHEA by the Numbers

115 Men's vocal cords vibrate about 115 times per second.

200 Women's vocal cords vibrate about 200 times per second.

20 There are 20 rings of cartilage in the trachea.

Diagrams of the Larynx and Trachea

A structure called the thyroid cartilage protects the larynx and sticks out at the front of the throat. The thyroid cartilage is larger in males than in females. It is also known as the Adam's apple.

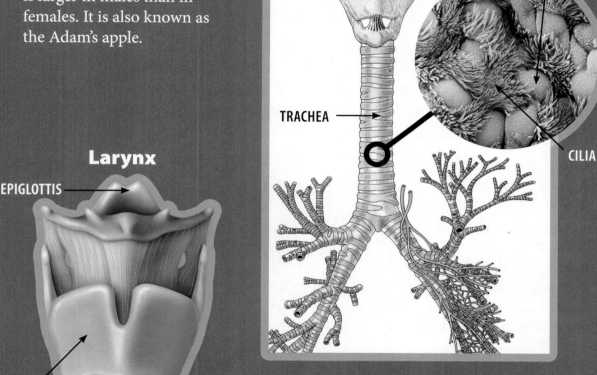

Trachea

CELLS THAT PRODUCE MUCUS

TRACHEA

CILIA

Larynx

EPIGLOTTIS

THYROID CARTILAGE

MUSCLES

TRACHEA

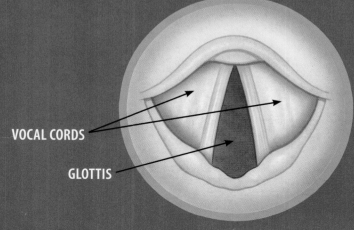

Vocal Cords, Open

VOCAL CORDS

GLOTTIS

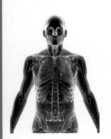

The Bronchi and Lungs

The two bronchi that enter the lungs are similar in structure to the trachea. They have stiff cartilage walls to keep the air passages open. They also have mucous membranes and cilia to continue removing dust and other particles from air entering the lungs.

Each tube is called a bronchus. Within a lung, the bronchus first branches into smaller tubes called secondary bronchi. These divide into still-smaller airways called tertiary bronchi. The tertiary bronchi then separate into bronchioles. In turn, these divide into even smaller tubes call terminal bronchioles, which have the alveoli at their ends.

Location of the Lungs

A thin membrane surrounds each lung and attaches the lung to the chest cavity. The membrane also allows the lungs to expand during breathing. The lungs are not exactly the same size.

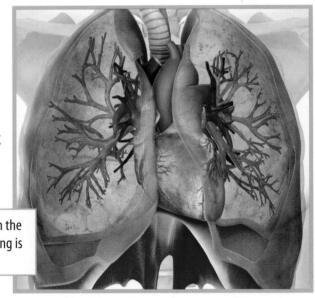

Because most of the heart is on the left side of the body, the left lung is smaller than the right one.

The BRONCHI AND LUNGS by the Numbers

2/3
Two-thirds of the heart is on the left side of the chest.

300
The lungs can hold about 300 cubic inches (5L) of air.

30,000
Each lung has about 30,000 bronchioles.

Diagram of the Bronchi and Lungs

The lungs are separated into divisions called lobes.
The smaller left lung has two lobes. The right lung has three.

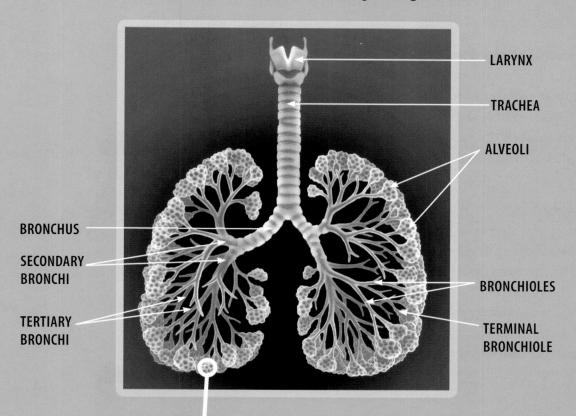

LARYNX

TRACHEA

ALVEOLI

BRONCHUS

SECONDARY BRONCHI

TERTIARY BRONCHI

BRONCHIOLES

TERMINAL BRONCHIOLE

Alveoli

Lobes of the Lungs

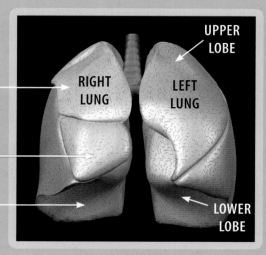

UPPER LOBE

RIGHT LUNG

LEFT LUNG

UPPER LOBE

MIDDLE LOBE

LOWER LOBE

LOWER LOBE

Keeping Healthy

The respiratory system is important to the health of the body. Therefore, people need to take care of their lungs and airways. Eating a healthful diet, getting regular exercise, and avoiding harmful habits keep the respiratory system working at its best.

Healthful Foods

The human body needs vitamins and other **nutrients** to build and maintain tissues. These include the tissues that are part of the respiratory system. It is also important to drink plenty of water every day.

Exercise

Regular exercise, especially outdoors in fresh air, is good for the respiratory system. During strenuous activity, such as biking, running, or swimming, the body's muscles need more oxygen. Therefore, the lungs need to take in more air.

Exercise makes the lungs stronger and able to hold more air.

60 MINUTES

The amount of exercise people should try to get every day.

VITAMIN-RICH FOODS

FRUIT

CARROTS

STRING BEANS

Healthful Lifestyle

Smoking damages tissues of the respiratory system and can lead to serious diseases such as lung cancer. Doctors recommend that people do not smoke. It is important to avoid breathing in other harmful substances, as well. People who work with chemicals or other materials that give off fumes need to wear masks to protect the airways. Home heating systems should be cleaned on a regular basis to make sure no harmful substances build up inside them.

Respiratory System Diseases

Some respiratory diseases are **inherited**. Other illnesses have environmental causes. The common cold, caused by a virus, is the most common illness of the respiratory system. Symptoms, which often last only a few days, include coughing, headache, runny nose, sneezing, and a sore throat.

HEALTHY AIRWAY

AIRWAY OF A PERSON WITH ASTHMA

Asthma is a long-term disease that causes airways to narrow and tighten, making it difficult to breathe. There is no cure for asthma, but the disease can be controlled.

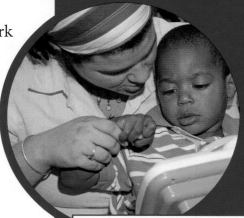

HIGH RISK

Almost 90 percent of lung cancer cases are related to smoking.

Cystic fibrosis is an inherited disease. It causes the body's mucus to be too thick and sticky, blocking airways and making breathing difficult.

Studying the Respiratory System

Today, several types of medical professionals study and treat diseases of the respiratory system. However, people have been studying the human body and its systems since ancient times.

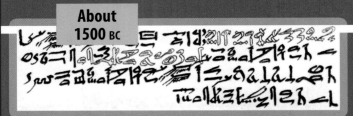

In Egypt, the Ebers Papyrus describes breathing treatments for asthma.

UNDERSTANDING OXYGEN

1910 Danish scientist August Krogh demonstrates that the blood delivers oxygen to body tissues.

The German physician Gustav Killian performs the first **bronchoscopy**.

1897

1963

Doctor James Hardy of the University of Mississippi performs the first human lung **transplant**.

1986

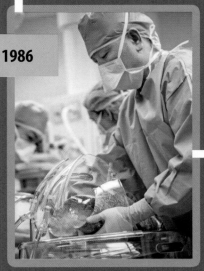

Surgeon Joel D. Cooper successfully performs the first transplant operation that replaces both lungs.

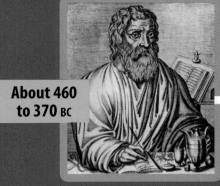

About 460 to 370 BC

The Greek physician Hippocrates conducts studies of the human body.

1200s AD

The Arab physician Ibn Al-Nafis proposes the theory that the blood must pass through the lungs before the heart pumps it around the body.

1816

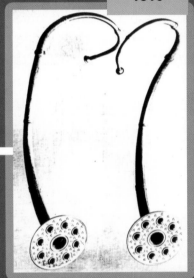

In France, Rene T. H. Laennec invents the **stethoscope**.

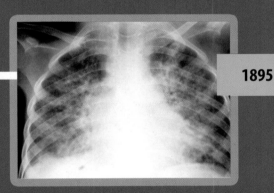

1895

German scientist Wilhelm Roentgen discovers X-rays, which doctors soon begin using to see structures inside the body.

1989

A team of scientists discovers the **gene** that causes cystic fibrosis.

2014

Discoveries by researchers at the Mayo Clinic may lead to treatment that could keep a form of lung cancer from developing in the human body.

Working Together

No system in the human body works alone. All the systems must work together to keep people healthy. The respiratory system works closely with several other systems in the body.

The Lungs and the Heart

The heart and lungs are connected through a part of the cardiovascular system called the pulmonary circulation. Blood that has picked up carbon dioxide from tissues in various parts of the body returns to the right side of the heart. The heart then pumps this blood into two vessels called the pulmonary arteries. One artery goes to each lung, where gas exchange takes place. Blood that is now oxygen-rich is returned to the left side of the heart by the pulmonary veins. The heart then pumps this blood throughout the body. In this way, the body's tissues receive the oxygen they need to function.

Breathing becomes deeper and more rapid when a person exercises, and the heart rate increases. In this way, the lungs and heart deliver more oxygen to the body's muscles.

70 The number of times, on average, the heart sends blood to the lungs each minute when a person is not exercising.

Muscles and Breathing

The respiratory system works with the body's muscular system. The intercostal muscles move the ribs as a person inhales and exhales. A set of muscles called the external intercostals raises the ribs, which increases the size of the chest cavity. This allows the lungs to expand and fill with air. A second set of muscles called the internal intercostals lowers the ribs. This reduces the size of the chest cavity and helps force air out of the lungs when a person exhales.

11 EACH
The number of external and internal intercostal muscles.

Within the body's muscles are structures that notice how active the muscles are. These structures then send signals to the brain, which speeds up breathing and heart rate.

More Than One

The nervous system has an important role in regulating breathing. The brain sends signals to the diaphragm and intercostal muscles that control when these muscles contract and relax. Nerve cells in the cardiovascular system monitor the amount of oxygen in the blood. If the oxygen content is too low, the nervous system sends signals to the respiratory system to breathe more often and more deeply.

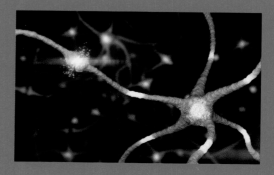

Careers

Several careers in health care involve working with patients who have respiratory system problems. Before considering a career, it is important to research options and learn about the educational requirements. It is also important to understand what the day-to-day work involves.

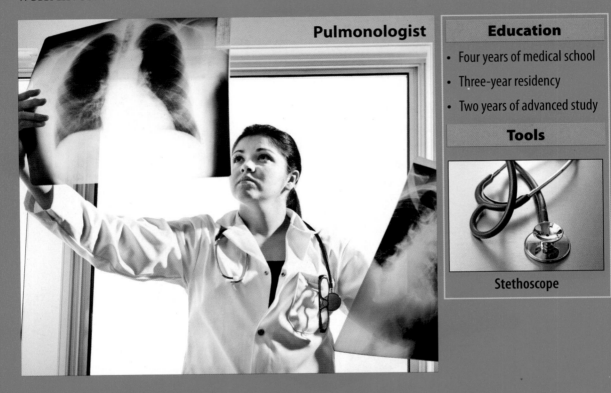

Pulmonologist

Education
- Four years of medical school
- Three-year residency
- Two years of advanced study

Tools

Stethoscope

Pulmonologists are doctors who specialize in treating disorders of the lungs and other parts of the respiratory system. They usually work with patients who have breathing problems, but they also treat sleep disorders, severe allergies, and other lung conditions. Pulmonologists work in hospitals, emergency care centers, and medical clinics.

Education
Pulmonologists earn a bachelor's degree, often in science or mathematics. This is followed by medical school, a **residency** program, and additional study of respiratory diseases.

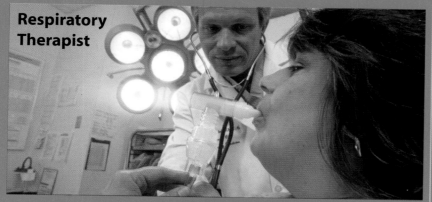

Respiratory Therapist

Education

- Two-year college degree
- Advanced degree
- Respiratory therapist license

Tools

Respirator

Respiratory therapists provide care to patients with breathing difficulties. They may also perform tests to collect information about the type of respiratory problem a person has. Respiratory therapists work in hospitals, rehabilitation centers, long-term care facilities, and private practices. Some respiratory therapists make in-home visits.

Education

Respiratory therapists often receive their training while earning a two-year college degree. They also can continue their education, obtaining a bachelor's or master's degree. Graduates must obtain a license.

Medical Imaging Technologist

Education

- Two-year college degree
- Specialized training
- Licensing examination

Tools

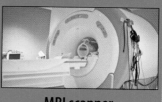

MRI scanner

Medical imaging technologists operate equipment such as magnetic resonance imaging (MRI) and X-ray machines. These devices produce images of organs within the body, such as the lungs. Doctors use these images to help determine a patient's illness and the best treatment for it.

Education

Medical imaging technologists obtain a two-year college degree and then may go on to specialized training in a particular field of medicine. They must pass an examination to receive a license.

The Respiratory System Quiz

Test your knowledge of the respiratory system by answering these questions. The answers are provided below for easy reference.

1 About how many bronchioles does each lung contain?

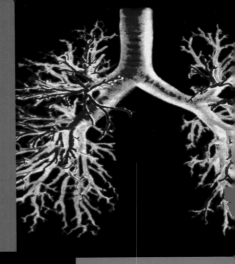

4 What is the name of the process that takes place in the lungs to bring oxygen into the blood and remove carbon dioxide from the blood?

7 What is the name of the hair-like structures that help to trap dust, pollen, and other materials in the airways?

2 When was the first lung transplant performed?

3 About how many alveoli are in a person's lungs?

5 What type of doctor specializes in diseases of the respiratory system?

6 Which structures in the larynx are important for producing sounds?

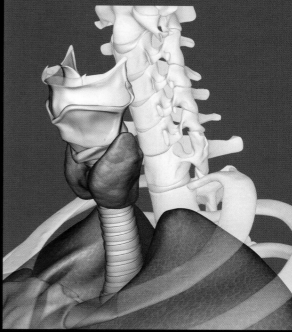

8 What is the process of breathing out called?

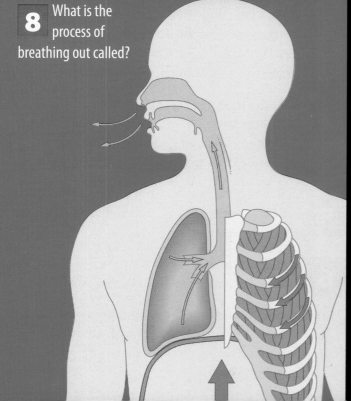

9 Who invented the stethoscope?

10 Which muscle that is important for breathing separates the chest from the abdomen?

Activity

You can build a model that will show how the respiratory system works. Using the model, you will be able to see how the diaphragm helps the breathing process.

BEFORE YOU START, YOU WILL NEED:

half-gallon (2-L) plastic bottle
scissors
small balloon
plastic drinking straw
rubber band
small piece of clay
ruler
small plastic bag
roll of clear tape

Build a Lung Model

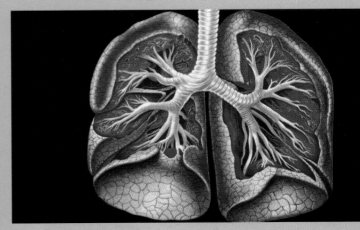

1 With an adult's help, cut the plastic bottle in half with scissors, so that one part has the bottle opening. Dispose of the bottom half.

2 Place the balloon on the end of the straw and secure it with a rubber band.

3 Make a hole through the clay, and poke the straw through it. Be careful not to plug the straw with the clay. Make sure at least 3 inches (8 cm) of straw is sticking through the clay.

4 Place the straw through the mouth of the bottle so that the straw is sticking out of the bottle and the balloon is hanging inside. Use the clay to secure the straw to the bottle and seal the edges.

5 Stretch the plastic bag across the opening at the bottom of the bottle half. Secure the plastic bag with tape.

6 Pull down or push up on the stretched plastic bag and watch what happens to the balloon.

Your model shows how the diaphragm's contracting and relaxing helps the lungs fill with air during inhalation and empty during exhalation.

Key Words

blood vessels: tube-shaped structures that carry blood around the body

bronchoscopy: a medical procedure for examining the inside of the airways using a long flexible tube

cartilage: a strong but flexible type of tissue found in various parts of the body

cells: the smallest structures in the body able to perform the functions necessary for life

contracts: becomes smaller or shorter

diaphragm: a sheet of muscle tissue that helps with breathing and that is located between the chest and abdomen, which is below the chest

esophagus: the muscular tube through which foods and liquids travel from the mouth down to the stomach

gene: a tiny unit within a cell that affects how something in the body looks or functions

inherited: passed down from one's parents or relatives who lived before them

intercostal muscles: muscles located between the ribs that help with breathing

mucus: a thick liquid produced by certain parts of the body

nutrients: substances that are needed by the body to stay healthy

organs: parts of the body that perform special functions

pollen: tiny particles produced by plants that may cause hay fever or other reactions in people who have certain allergies

residency: a period, often soon after graduation from medical school, when a doctor receives advanced training by practicing under the supervision of more experienced doctors

stethoscope: a medical instrument used to listen to sounds inside a patient's body

tissue: a structure in the body made up of the same type of cells

transplant: a type of surgery in which an organ from one person is placed in another person's body

Index

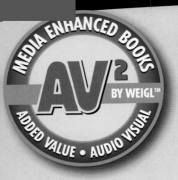

Log on to www.av2books.com

AV² by Weigl brings you media enhanced books that support active learning. Go to www.av2books.com, and enter the special code found on page 2 of this book. You will gain access to enriched and enhanced content that supplements and complements this book. Content includes video, audio, weblinks, quizzes, a slide show, and activities.

AV² Online Navigation

Book Pages
AV² pages directly correspond to pages in the book.

Key Words
Study vocabulary, and complete a matching word activity.

Quizzes
Test your knowledge.

Slide Show
View images and captions, and prepare a presentation.

Audio
Listen to sections o the book read alou

Video
Watch informative video clips.

Embedded Weblinks
Gain additional information for research.

Try This!
Complete activities and hands-on experiments.

AV² was built to bridge the gap between print and digital. We encourage you to tell us what you like and what you want to see in the future.

Sign up to be an AV² Ambassador at www.av2books.com/ambassador.

Due to the dynamic nature of the Internet, some of the URLs and activities provided as part of AV² by Weigl may have changed or ceased to exist. AV² by Weigl accepts no responsibility for any such changes. All media enhanced books are regularly monitored to update addresses and sites in a timely manner. Contact AV² by Weigl at 1-866-649-3445 or av2books@weigl.com with any questions, comments, or feedback.